= *The* =

CHARLESTON & HAMBURG

= *The* =
CHARLESTON
&HAMBURG

A South Carolina Railroad and an American Legacy

Thomas Fetters

Charleston   London
History
PRESS

Published by The History Press
Charleston, SC 29403
www.historypress.net

Copyright © 2008 by Thomas Fetters
All rights reserved

Cover design by Natasha Momberger.

First published 2008

Manufactured in the United Kingdom

ISBN 978.1.59629.420.2

Library of Congress Cataloging-in-Publication Data

Fetters, Thomas T.
The Charleston & Hamburg : a South Carolina railroad and an American legacy / Thomas Fetters.
p. cm.
ISBN-13: 978-1-59629-420-2 (alk. paper)
1. Charleston & Hamburg Railroad--History. 2. Railroads--South
Carolina--History. I. Title.
HE2791.C5263F48 2008
385.09757--dc22

2007046934

*This book is dedicated to my two grandchildren,
Jake Conner and Ryan Conner. Both boys are imaginative
and creative and I expect great things from them.*

Contents

Acknowledgements

A ny manuscript that stretches back over fifty years relies on a multitude of sources and individuals who pitch in with information here and there. Certainly Mary Lehr—president of the Charleston Chapter of the National Railway Historical Society, who made a number of trips locally to search out sources of material—and Craig Meyer—editor of *TIES*, the quarterly of the Southern Railway Historical Society, who provided some photographs—earned special attention for their help.

I also need to acknowledge the assistance of nearly everyone else who in one way or another helped with material regarding the Charleston & Hamburg. It was a story that needed to be told in greater detail.

Introduction

This book was prepared over a very long time, beginning with gathering information as far back as the 1950s. It would be impossible to call out everyone who helped with the project over fifty years, but perhaps the sophomore class world history teacher at the High School of Charleston was the most important, because as a transfer student I had to take this class to graduate. We all were required to do a paper on Sergeant Jasper. Virtually unknown outside of the Charleston area, this valiant soldier protected the inlet between the Isle of Palms and Sullivan's Island on the Atlantic Coast from the invading British forces in the Revolutionary War period. This tidal inlet was treacherous and washed the Brits out to sea. I often rode over the bridge that connects the two islands and every time I doffed my hat, in imagination, to his gallant defense of the area. This teacher's assignment led directly to my quest to record the railroad history of the state of South Carolina in a very broad way to show the outside influences that bore on the railroads and how the railroads influenced the state's economy and progress.

I have worked on the history of South Carolina's railroads ever since, because the subject is not widely known and because it is fascinating in its own right.

Throughout the text, the numbers used in the roster lists of locomotives are my own. The locomotives were not assigned numbers by the Charleston & Hamburg Rail Road. Rebuilt locomotives have been given number and letter designations, as they are not new in the sense of a totally new machine.

A Friend in Need...
Is a Friend Indeed!

In the early 1800s, Charleston shipped three staples abroad: cotton to England, lumber to the West Indies and rice to southern Europe. From 1817 to 1824, Charleston held a monopoly on steamboat trade on the Savannah River, much to the disgust of the city of Savannah, which served only as a refueling station for the steamers en route to Charleston with bales of cotton stacked all about the decks. But Savannah soon had its own fleet of steamboats plying their way up and down the Savannah, and it was not long before the Charleston boats found it too expensive to compete. With the monopoly broken, Savannah became the primary shipping port for goods traveling down the Savannah River from Augusta, bringing both Georgia and South Carolina crops and other goods to that port.

Charleston found itself facing economic disaster. William Aiken and Alexander Black, two prominent Charlestonians, felt that a solution might be a new development being tried experimentally in England: a railed road.

Instead of laying a ten-foot-wide pathway of split logs and planks that would allow passage to farm wagons, stage coaches and other wheeled carriages, a railed road could be only five feet wide with only two strips or "rails" supported by cross members elevated on pilings to prevent flooding in swampy areas. Special coaches or carriages with flanged wheels would be guided by the rails and commerce would be dependent on the owner of the rails and the specially designed carriages. The cost of building such a railed road was minimal when compared to the State Road that was still under construction between Columbia and Charleston in the treacherous swamp areas near the Santee River.

HAMBURG: THE GOAL

Where to build such a novel road? Aiken suggested that Hamburg, South Carolina, just across the Savannah River from Augusta, Georgia, would be an excellent terminal to regain the trade lost to the Savannah steamboats. Hamburg had been settled in 1820 by Henry Schultz and had been formally founded in 1821 near the cotton warehouse Schultz had built to consolidate shipments to Charleston via the Savannah River.

William Aiken, one of Schultz's loyal friends, felt that constructing a new railed road through to Hamburg could trump Savannah's use of steamboats on the river and reinstate Hamburg as the principal trade center, to the discomfort of both Augusta and its shipping partner on the coast.

The Charleston & Hamburg

1827—The Charleston & Hamburg Charter

With the backing of several prominent Charleston merchants, the Charleston & Hamburg Rail Road was chartered on December 19, 1827, for Alexander Black, who proposed to build and operate a railed road from Charleston to Hamburg, Columbia and Camden. Each of these cities promised to provide access to the agricultural goods of western Carolina and Georgia, central Carolina and to northern Carolina and North Carolina, respectively. This new company was greeted with cheers, but there was a tremendous amount of work necessary to get the line into operation.

1828—The South Carolina Canal & Rail Road Charter

On January 8, 1828, a number of Charlestonians who were intent on supporting Black's railed road found that his Charleston & Hamburg Rail Road had been granted a charter based on the previous charters for turnpike and toll bridge companies. These people redesigned a new form of charter for canals and railroads and the South Carolina Canal and Rail Road was granted this new form of charter on January 30, 1828. This charter was so much broader in scope that the C&HRR became only one of several operations authorized in the SCC&RR paper. The railroad retained the identity of Charleston & Hamburg Rail Road. Elias Horry, the president of the SCC&RR Company, referred to the railroad as the C&HRR in his letters and reports.

Horatio Allen

The most influential man in railroad circles was a Yankee, Horatio Allen, born in Schenectady, New York, on May 10, 1802. Both an inventor and a civil engineer with a degree from Columbia College, which he received at twenty-one, Allen became the chief engineer for the Delaware & Hudson Canal Company, which sent him to England in 1828 to buy several locomotives for the company. Allen met George Stephenson, purchased a rather crude, barrel-boilered machine and had it shipped back to Pennsylvania. There, at Honesdale, he assembled the first steam locomotive to operate in America, a primitive machine named the Stourbridge Lion. While the machine ran well with Allen himself at the throttle on August 9, 1829, in several test runs, it was decided that it was inferior to horsepower. The company then had planks laid between the rails, and horses were brought in to move the cars of coal. Allen was the first person to operate a locomotive in the Western Hemisphere.

Allen then went to Charleston, where he took the position of chief engineer for the Charleston & Hamburg Rail Road. He deserves the credit for convincing the company to look strongly at the attributes of the steam locomotive.

The stockholders formed the South Carolina Canal & Rail Road Company on May 12, 1828, making it the second company in the United States formed to commercially transport passengers and general freight. Five days later, Horatio Allen met with the company to discuss the kind of road to be built and the best power to be used to move the cars. This was, in his opinion, the steam locomotive.

Allen told of the Liverpool & Manchester Company in England that had decided to install a series of stationary steam engines "positioned every one to three miles apart, which, through long ropes, were to draw the trains from one engine to the other." This method is, of course, utilized by cable-car transit systems that move cars with cable ropes powered by a central cable house. He also reported that while the "Baltimore & Ohio Railroad Company had sixteen miles in operation by horsepower," they had been advised by English engineers to use horsepower to move the cars. Allen made his point that "there was no reason to believe that the breed of horses would be materially improved, but that the present breed of locomotives was to furnish a power of which no one knew its limit, and which would far exceed its present performances." The directors of the Charleston & Hamburg Rail Road, "before they left their seats, passed the resolution unanimously that the South Carolina railroad should be built solely for locomotive power."

Contemporary papers consistently refer to the company as the Charleston & Hamburg Rail Road and it is by this name that it was popularly known. An excellent example is the report by William Howard, U.S. Civil Engineer, published in Charleston in 1829: "Report on the Charleston & Hamburg Rail-Road to the President and Directors of the South Carolina Canal and Rail Road Company."

1828—THE FIRST C&HRR SURVEY

Several surveys were made in 1828 and 1829 under the direction of William Aiken, the president of the C&HRR. One was conducted by Charles Parker and Robert K. Payne, who examined a potential route from February 20 to June 12 of 1828. The two men left Charleston by carriage on Sunday, February 24 at 11:45 a.m. and "arrived at the Six Mile House at one o'clock, where Mr. Arnot, the keeper, was requested to provide dinner as soon as possible." Payne paid Arnot $1.62 for the meals. (There were several inns along the State Road that were known by the distance back to the corner of Broad Street and Meeting Street, the financial center of the city. Six Mile House was six miles from that intersection.) Parker and Payne then left at 2:15 p.m. and "arrived at Ashley Ferry at twenty minutes after 3." Here Payne paid the $0.50 fare for the two men. The Ashley Ferry was later more popularly known as Bee's Ferry, after the proprietor. This was located on the Ashley River where the current CSX Railroad Bridge crosses the river.

"From town to Ashley Ferry the soil is sandy and unsupported by any firm clay. Beyond said ferry there is a firm and tenacious layer a little below the surface of the soil. It rained until 12 o'clock this day but not afterward." Evidently the men waited until the rain ended before beginning their journey. The firm and tenacious layer that was mentioned was perhaps the first published mention of the phosphate strata that lay only inches below the soil west of the Ashley River. This material was later recognized as being worth a fortune and led to a revival of Charleston's economy after the War Between the States.

The two men stayed overnight at Mrs. Chandler's, which was twenty-five miles from Charleston. They "put us up for the night, took supper and lodging, for which Payne paid $6.50 including the toll for Slan's Bridge." Slan's Bridge is directly west of Summerville and crosses the Ashley River. This information lets us see that the two men had used Ashley River Road from Bee's Ferry, passing Drayton Hall, Magnolia Plantation, Runnymede, Millbrook and Middleton Place to reach Bacon's Bridge Crossroads. Only a mile or two beyond was Mrs. Chandler's inn.

Monday the men were up early and headed west. "Started this morning at half past 6 and arrived at Givhan's Ferry at half before ten. Road bad and sloppy. The declivity to Slans Bridge is sudden near Mrs. Chandlers, but the ascent on the other side is more gradual. Breakfasted at Givhan's Ferry, Mr. Payne paid $2.81." Givhan's Ferry allowed travelers to cross the Edisto River.

The men then headed west to Raysor's, north of Walterboro, fifteen miles away from the ferry where they stopped for dinner. They then continued on to William's Tavern, where they stayed the night. The road from Givhan's Ferry to William's Tavern was described as "tolerably level, though very sloppy and bad. The weather during the whole day was clear and fine."

On Tuesday, the men left at 7:30 a.m. and crossed "six considerable valleys some from 15 to 20 feet deep and several hundred yards wide, being **considerable obstacles to a railway**." They rode on to Walker's, some six miles away, and arrived at 9:00 a.m., but could not get breakfast there. They then rode on for twelve miles to Trotties, where they arrived at 11:00 a.m. Here they had breakfast and Payne paid $2.25 for the meal and care for the horses.

They continued on until 5:30 p.m., when they arrived at Mrs. Hartruch's, some sixteen miles from Trotties. They had managed to ride twenty-eight miles over bad road. Here they had dinner and Payne paid for supper, lodging and breakfast for $6.50.

On Thursday, the survey work began in earnest. Some 180 wooden pegs were made with hatchets and two men were employed at two dollars a day to measure a route to Hamburg from "The Forks" at Wooley's, where one road headed north to Edgefield Courthouse and the other headed west to Hamburg. The team followed the Hamburg road using surveyors' chains and tables from a book, *Wyld's Practical Surveyors*, which had "tables of the earth's curvature calculated to the thousandth part of a foot at the end of every chain." This correction permitted more accurate measurement of the length across the land.

After little more than three weeks on the road, the men completed the survey on March 13 and turned in their expenses. Meals and lodging came in at $148.75. Renting two saddle horses for twenty days had cost $60. Hiring two servants for twenty days was $40. The nine days leading up to the survey had expenses of $180, with the carriage billing at $85. Overall, the "total expense for the expedition was $964.75."

The diary kept by Parker in his notebook is a window to a world where the roads could be traveled at six miles an hour on horseback, and noted to be "sloppy and very bad." The improvement in travel time gained by building the State Road with planks on logs takes on greater significance, yet this remarkable improvement was to be reduced considerably by the promised railroad.

Parker and Payne wrote a report to the chairman of the Committee of Railroads, Timothy Ford, that "upon examination we found the country between Hamburg and the Horse Pen Pond to be as follows. The bridge over Horse Creek is upon a level with Hamburg. The summit of the ridge along the public road leading from Mosely's to Hamburg is to be found at Joseph Coslahan's settlement, situated two miles from Mosely's and seventeen from Hamburg." The conclusion was that Coslahan's was 375 feet above the Horse Creek and that a line rising at 26 feet to the mile would be needed to cover the 14 miles in length. They suggested that a stationary steam engine or a source of horsepower be used to pull the cars up the hillside. We shall see that this survey was very accurate, and indeed the solution proposed by Parker and Payne proved to be the solution to conquering the descent at Aiken.

1829—Two Other C&H Surveys

Another survey was completed on August 27 of 1829. It proposed that the line would proceed up the Charleston Neck between the Ashley and Cooper Rivers, then turn northwest and cross the Ashley River above Dorchester near the river's source (probably near Slan's Bridge) and proceed to Givhan's Ferry on the Edisto River. After crossing the Edisto, the line would follow the natural ridge on to Horse Pen Pond, 94 miles from Charleston. It would then turn south to Hamburg, following the creek to reach Hamburg. The gauge was to be $4\frac{1}{2}$ feet between the rails and the surveyed length was to be $149\frac{1}{2}$ miles.

Horatio Allen decided to re-survey the route after being hired as the chief engineer of the company. His alternative route ran directly up the Charleston Neck, straight to Summerville and then west to a much easier crossing of the smaller, upstream Edisto, well above Givhan's Ferry. This line ran to the source of Horse Creek and then south to Hamburg and provided a route of only 135 miles with a much easier topography to conquer.

1829—The Flanged Wheel Experiments

The first two years that the company was in existence were devoted to discussions on the route to be taken to reach the cities of interest, the construction methods to be used and the propulsion for the trains. Experts of the day declared that the railroad would kill all of its passengers, since anyone traveling at thirty miles per hour could not breathe and would expire from suffocation.

Fearful of being held up to ridicule, the company began its first tests in relative secrecy. A section of track, 150 feet long, was built in the middle of cobblestoned Wentworth

Street in February of 1829. The company then obtained a small four-wheel flat car with flanged wheels for the test. The car was loaded with forty-seven bales of cotton, a formidable load. A single mule was hitched to the car and the watchers were stunned to see the animal pull this load along the street with ease. No one had ever seen a mule haul even a quarter of this load; thus the practical efficiency of the flanged wheels on track was ably demonstrated.

A second track segment that was 170 feet long was constructed in April at Chisolm's Wharf. This track had similar small four-wheel cars that were used to move the flat iron straps for the track of the C&H from the wharf to the street at the wharf's end. With some five hundred tons of iron strap on hand, the stockholders met in June of 1829 to authorize an advance of $100,000 as a loan to provide the financial incentive for the company.

1829—THE PROPULSION EXPERIMENTS

Several experimental cars were tested in 1829, including two manual handcars of different designs and a treadmill horse car called the Flying Dutchman. This last machine was built by Thomas Dotterer and Christian Detmold of the Eason & Dotterer firm (described below). The new car was entered into a contest held by the directors of the railroad on September 14, 1829, and was judged to be the best entry. Allen said later that the car "worked on an endless chain platform. When this horse-power locomotive was completed and tested upon the road, it carried twelve passengers at the rate of twelve miles an hour." Eason & Dotterer was awarded a first prize of $200 (a purchasing power equal to several thousand current dollars).

1830—CONSTRUCTION BEGINS

Construction of the C&HRR began at the outskirts of the city of Charleston in January of 1830. The railroad, as welcome as it may have been, was not permitted to operate within the city of Charleston. The tracks, therefore, began at Line Street in the alleyway between King Street and Meeting Street, about two and a quarter miles northwest of the main intersection in the city, Meeting and Broad Streets (known today as the corner of the four governments). Each corner of that intersection today is marked by a major building representing the law of the city (city hall), the state, the federal government (U.S. Post Office) or God (a church).

Allen revised the track gauge from the proposed four and a half feet to five foot between the rails for greater stability of the equipment while in motion. Wooden piles with an eight- by eight-inch-square section were driven into the soft ground six feet apart across the line and seven feet apart along the line to support cross stringers. The rails were wooden beams, six by nine inches in section, covered with strap iron strips for the wheels to run upon, and the rails were elevated at least a foot above the surface of the wet, marshy ground. Where the ground was dry, the "sills" beneath the rails were to be sunk into the ground four to five inches with four to five inches above ground. When curves were encountered, an L-shaped flange rail of iron was used to protect against the wear of the wheel flange, which was to be inside the rails.

The Charleston & Hamburg Rail Road terminal at Line Street included a rudimentary station as well as the required terminal facilities to house, service and repair the equipment. The facility was located just to the west of Meeting Street, which itself was the extension of the State Road into town.

The C&H tracks extended northwest between Meeting and King Streets until they left the urban environment and entered an undeveloped, marshy area laced with saltwater creeks. The city's cemeteries were in this district, and there were several significant landmarks along the way that were originally established to support the State Road. Five Mile House and Ten Mile House, named for the distance back to Meeting and Broad Streets, were able to provide meals and lodging to the travelers on the original road.

1830—Another Innovative Rail Car

The company had a full mile of track in place by mid-March of 1830. This allowed the C&H to work with another type of experimental car. This was a small two-axle wagon with a single mast supporting a sail about five by nine feet in size. On March 20, 1830, thirteen people were propelled at some fifteen miles per hour along the existing line, along with three tons of freight. After several minutes of good sailing, a gust of wind blew mast, sail and rigging overboard together with the wagon, and the passengers came tumbling after. Luckily, no one was injured in the mishap and the car was quickly re-railed. A jury-rigged mast was soon set in place and the car "flew" up and down the mile of mainline for the rest of the day.

The *Charleston Courier* reported the experiment in this way:

> *Fifteen gentlemen got on board and flew oft at the rate of twelve to fourteen miles an hour. Thirteen persons and three tons of iron were carried about ten miles an hour. The preparations for sailing were very hastily got up, and of course were not of the best kind, but owing to this circumstance, the experiment afforded high sport. The wind blew very fresh from about north east which, as a sailor would say, was "abeam," and would drive the car either way with equal speed. When going at the rate of about twelve miles an hour and loaded with fifteen passengers, the mast went by the board with the sail and rigging attached, carrying with them several of the crew. The wreck was described by several friendly shipmasters who kindly rendered assistance in rigging a jury mast, and the car was again soon put under way. During the afternoon the wind changed so as to bring it nearly ahead when going in any direction; but this did not stop the sport as it was ascertained that the car would sail within four points of the winch. We understand it is intended by some of our seamen to rig a car properly and shortly to exhibit their skill in managing a vessel on land.*

Allen even traveled north to Baltimore, Maryland, where he saw a test track of the Baltimore & Ohio Rail Road, where the Yankees were evaluating a small steam engine on wheels that was proving successful. He observed that steam engines were rapidly being adapted for ocean steamers to cross the Atlantic. These new steamships, revolutionizing the time needed to cross the high seas, were the inspiration for dependable cheap power for the railed road. Allen set aside his experiments with sailed cars that could become becalmed when he saw that windless days had no effect on the ocean steamships. Similarly, he set aside his thoughts of horsepower, as there was no need for stables, and teams of fresh horses stationed along the right-of-way and the constant problem of supplying fodder for the animals. The steam locomotive could use scrap wood from the forests to feed it and it could drink from the dark waters of the swamps that could sicken a horse.

While the B&O claims to be the first railroad in America, it continued to test locomotives well after the Charleston & Hamburg began regular scheduled trips at the end of 1830. In fact, the railroad determined that the steam locomotive was not the best way to run a railroad. When the B&O finally began regular service over its line using a steam locomotive, the C&H was well on its way to becoming the longest railroad in the world.

ROBERT YOUNG HAYNE

Robert Young Hayne was born on November 10, 1791, at Pon Pon Plantation (Pon Pon was the Indian name for the Edisto River) in Colleton District, west of Charleston. He went to private schools and studied law, which led to his passing the bar in 1812 at age twenty-one. The War of 1812 fell on the Lowcountry with the sudden British invasion of Charleston and British troops scouring the countryside looking for American forces. Hayne rose to the rank of captain of the Charleston Cadet Riflemen, and then was appointed as quartermaster general of South Carolina in 1814. He served in the South Carolina House of Representatives from 1814 to 1818 and was Speaker of the House in 1818. He then served a term as state attorney general from 1818 to 1822, when he was elected to the United States Senate. Hayne was elected for a second term in 1828 as an Andrew Jackson Republican, but resigned in December of 1832 to become governor of South Carolina for two years. He then became mayor of Charleston for a term from 1835 to 1837, while promoting and serving as president of the Louisville, Cincinnati & Charleston Rail Road. The financial panic of 1837 ended the possibility of raising funds for the railroad. He died on September 24, 1839, at age forty-eight and was buried at St Michael's Churchyard in Charleston. Hayne had a unique career and seems to have been the right man at the right time as he moved from position to position. There is no doubt that he was the most influential man in the state from 1822 until his death in 1839.

1. Best Friend of Charleston (0-4-0)

The steam engine, which was used to a limited extend overseas in England and was being tested in Maryland and Pennsylvania, was selected by Horatio Allen as the most promising way to operate trains to Hamburg. The SCC&RR had no funds at hand for such an unproven concept, and a local Charleston businessman, E.L. Miller, provided the $4,000 to purchase a locomotive, on the basis that the C&H would buy the machine from him if it proved to meet the requirements. Miller had preliminary plans and specifications prepared by Christian Detmold of the Eason & Dotterer firm.

A basic design was prepared for the West Point Foundry, located at Beach and West Streets in New York City. Construction was started in the early summer of 1830 on the 0-4-0 vertical boiler Best Friend of Charleston, the first practical steam locomotive built in America. David Cashew, who had assembled the Stourbridge Lion when it arrived from England and tested it in the West Point Foundry yard, reported that the "Best Friend was a four wheel engine, all four wheels drivers. Two inclined cylinders at an angle, working down on a double crank, inside of the frame, with the wheels outside of the frame, each wheel connecting together outside, with outside rods. The wheels were iron hub, wooden spokes and fellows, with iron tire and iron web and pins in the wheels to connect the outside rods to."

Cashew continued,

> The boiler was a vertical one, in the form of an old fashioned porter-bottle, the furnace at the bottom surrounded with water and all filled inside with what we called teats running out from the sides and top with alternate stays to support the crown of the furnace; the smoke and gas passing out through the sides at several point into an outside jacket which had the chimney on it. The boiler sat in the center of the four wheels with the connecting rods running by to come into the crank shaft. The cylinders were about six inches in the bore and sixteen inches stroke. Wheels [were] about four and a half feet in diameter. The whole machine weighed about four and a half tons. It was shipped to Charleston, South Carolina for the Charleston & Hamburg Rail Road, in the fall of 1830 and was put upon that road during the winter.

The machine was then disassembled and shipped down the Atlantic Coast on the *Niagara* and subsequently arrived in Charleston on October 23, 1830. The *Charleston Courier* wrote, "We understand that the steam engine intended for our road is on board the ship *Niagara*, which arrived in the offing last night." At about the same time, the Tom Thumb, an experimental locomotive built for the Baltimore & Ohio in August of 1830, was given several trial runs. This locomotive was never intended for actual commercial service, but was merely for a demonstration of the potential of the steam locomotive.

The Best Friend, which arrived in parts, was taken to the shops of Thomas Dotterer and his partner, Eason. Under the supervision of his foreman, Julius D. Petsch, and assisted by Nicholas W. Darrell, "a young man just out of his time in their workshops," the engine was reassembled and then prepared for testing on the tracks.

The four-and-a-half-ton locomotive could develop only six horsepower. All four of the wheels were drivers connected together with outside rods and driven by a double crank inside the frame pushed by two six-inch bore inclined cylinders mounted at the front of the engines frame that had a sixteen-inch stroke. The tires of the four-and-a-half-foot-diameter wheels were made of iron spread by hardwood spokes set into an iron hub on the axles.

The trial run of November 2, 1830, which followed several earlier successful runs, was not so lucky. With young Darrell as engineer, E.L. Miller "accompanied by several gentlemen in a car made a trial trip." The Best Friend and the single car ran to the end of the line, but on returning "the forward wheel was sprung inward so much so as to leave the rail entirely and the engine, after proceeding about twenty feet, was stopped with both the front wheels off the rail and some of the spokes much injured." The engine crew, Darrell and a black fireman, suffered some bruises as they held onto the pitching platform.

John Degnon of 48 First Street in New York City claimed in a letter to *Scientific American* that he had "run the Best Friend for three months, or thereabouts, meanwhile giving Mr. Darrell the necessary instructions to qualify him for the post." Julius Petsch was asked if this was true and said the "statement is entirely incorrect." Petsch recalled that E.L. Miller had intended to bring "a competent person" with him to Charleston to assemble the machine and this was printed in the local Charleston newspapers. Petsch declined to assemble the Best Friend after seeing the comment in the paper, but "to please Mr. Dotterer, at last consented. I took Mr. Darrell to assist me. After erecting and putting the engine on the road, I ran it for three or four days, having Mr. Darrell with me all the time and then turned her over to him as engineer." Although an effort was made to have Degnon defend his statement, he died before being able to reply.

By the end of November 1830, five additional miles of track had been built northward up the Charleston peninsula to San Souci, a nearby community. Thus the stage was set for the grand experiment that would prove the worth of the locomotive and flanged carriages on rigid iron strap rails.

After a month of reworking the locomotive and replacing the wooden spokes with iron spoked wheels, the Best Friend made its next trial on December 9. The most successful trial was completed on December 14, when the locomotive pulled two fourteen-foot coaches with forty men at twenty miles per hour without an incident. With the completion of the trial runs in November and December, the results were judged to be a complete success. The C&HRR then purchased Miller's locomotive for use in regular service.

Contemporary drawings of the Best Friend show that the base of the boiler is within six inches of the rail top. A large steam pipe emerges from the boiler top and runs down to the platform. There is no seat for the engineer, who stands and uses a large upright lever to control the steam flow and as a consequence the speed of the train. There is a railing for the fireman to use as support. (A replica of the Best Friend was built by the Southern Railway in 1928 and has the bottom of the boiler at the level of the axle centerline. The steam pipe closely follows the contour of the boiler. There is a seat for

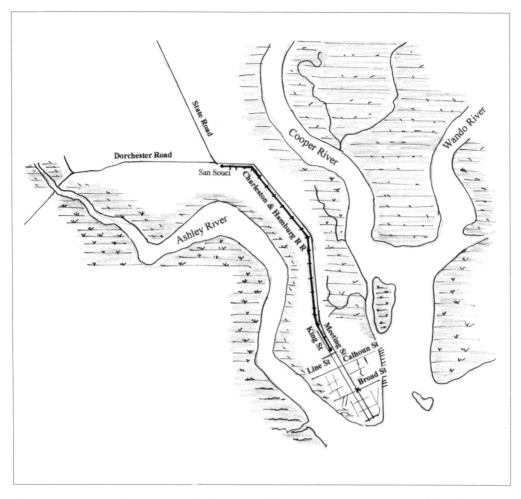

This map shows the original route of the first scheduled train in America, pulled by the Best Friend of Charleston, on Christmas Day, 1830. Departing from a station just north of Line Street, the train ran to San Souci at the Forks of Dorchester and State Roads. *Map by the author.*

the engineer and the control lever is low and close to the platform. There is no railing for the fireman. Curiously, the replica has an additional gasoline engine hidden under barrels on the tender, making the replica a form of articulated locomotive.)

On Christmas Eve of 1830, the Charleston papers contained the following announcement:

> *The public are respectfully informed that the Rail Road Company has purchased from Mr. E.L. Miller his locomotive steam engine and that it will hereafter be constantly employed in the transportation of passengers. The time of leaving the station in Line Street will be 8 o'clock, at 10AM, at 1 and half past three o'clock P.M. Parties may be accommodated by agreeing with the engineer. Great punctuality will be observed in the time of starting.*

The original Best Friend of Charleston lacked any safety railings or a seat for the engineer such as those used on the replicas built in the twentieth century, which had to provide for the safety of the operator. The two pistons are mounted by the driver who holds the tall throttle device to control the speed of the locomotive. Note that the drivers are connected by a rod to distribute the power to all four wheels. *Author's collection.*

Opening Day

On Christmas Day, Charlestonians saw the first regularly scheduled passenger train to operate in America pull away from the Line Street station. Operated by Nicholas W. Darrell as engineer, the train ran as far as San Souci that day and each day thereafter. The first trip was described enthusiastically by a sportswriter, Jockey of York.

Away we flew on the wings of the wind at the speed of 15 to 25 miles per hour, annihilating time and space, and like the renowned John Gilpin, leaving all the world behind. It was nine minutes, five and one fourth seconds since we started and we discovered ourselves beyond the forks of the State and Dorchester Roads. I swear by the spectacles I shall one day or other wear, that either the road or engine turned round like a top. [It passed the cars and] as each car came in front, it gave us three whiffs of steam. On our return, it again headed the column. We came to San Souci in quick time. Here we stopped to take up a recruiting party, darted forth like a live rocket, scattering sparks and flames on either side, passed over three saltwater creeks, hop, step and jump and landed us all at the Lines before any of us had time to determine whether or not it was prudent to be scared.

Jockey of York managed to describe the turntable at the end of the line and the passing of the locomotive past the passenger cars as it moved to the new front of the train.

Some 141 persons rode the first trip to San Souci, riding in two passenger cars. An additional flatcar was connected for the detachment of United States troops in the recruiting party and a small field cannon. Darrell retightened the bearing packing after the return, and the second trip left at 1:00 p.m. with 100 passengers and returned at 4:00 in two trips to bring some 200 passengers back to Line Street.

The first trips of the Best Friend over the railroad were reported around the world. While there were some misgivings by those with other theories on the best way to run a railroad, there was no denying that the Charleston & Hamburg had met the deadline and was completely satisfactory in its efforts. Here was the finest Christmas present a city ever received; truly the locomotive was to become the "Best Friend of Charleston."

1831–The First Year of Operation

Flush with success, the company quickly settled into a daily routine of running four trains up to San Souci and back. It was not long before a transfer depot was set up and freight, bound for Charleston on the State Road, was transferred to small freight cars and quickly delivered to the terminal at Line Street close by the heart of Charleston and the docks on the Cooper River. The company immediately realized that a second locomotive was needed.

STOCKHOLDERS' EXCURSION

One year after construction of the C&H track had begun, the South Carolina Canal & Rail Road Company held a stockholders' meeting to discuss the advances of the company through the year and the success of the Charleston & Hamburg daily service to San Souci. As a special benefit, the company arranged for a special train to be operated on January 15, 1831, for the enlightenment of the stockholders. The train had a flatcar with a small cannon cared for by three cadets from the local Citadel, followed by two regular passenger cars for the investors and their wives. Scheduled to run in the afternoon, the trip offset the normal run that ran later in the day.

The trip was made without incident and proved to be a great boost to the confidence of the men who were still a bit uneasy over the use of a steam locomotive to move a train over rails. It was clear, however, that the company could certainly use at least one more locomotive for sustained service without interruptions.

2. WEST POINT (0-4-0)

The overwhelming success of the Charleston & Hamburg trains led to the ordering and construction of a second locomotive. This became the first American locomotive built with a horizontal boiler. Named the West Point, it was ordered from the same West Point Foundry in New York as the Best Friend.

After it arrived from New York City on the *Lafayette*, the machine was set up and put into trial service. As the *Charleston Courier* put it:

The stockholders' special train of January 15, 1831, included a flatcar with a small cannon and three cadets from The Citadel, along with two cars to accommodate the investors and their wives. Nicholas Darrell served as engineer on the way to San Souci at the forks of Dorchester and State Roads. *Author's collection.*

By an amazing coincidence, the very same people, sitting in exactly the same positions, were later drawn by the artist, as riding behind the ten-ton English-built Portsmouth & Roanoke locomotive Raleigh a few years later. *Author's collection.*

On Saturday afternoon, March 5, 1831, the locomotive West Point underwent a trial of speed with the barrier car and four cars for passengers. There were 117 passengers aboard, of whom 50 were ladies in the four cars and 9 passengers on the engine tender with 6 bales of cotton on the barrier car. The trip to Five Mile House, two and ¾ miles, was completed in 11 minutes where the cars were stopped to oil the axles about two minutes. The two and a quarter miles to the forks of Dorchester Road were completed in 8 minutes.

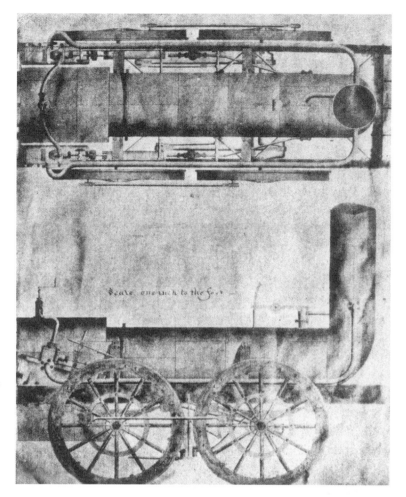

This appears to be the representation of the West Point as it was built. Its legend reports, "Original drawing of the 'West Point,' the second locomotive engine built for actual service on a railroad in the United States. Made for the South Carolina Rail Road A.D. 1830 to 1831 by the West Point Foundry Association." The original drawing is at the American Society of Civil Engineers at 33 W 39th Street in New York. *Author's collection.*

Contemporary drawings of the West Point exist that show a long, slim boiler with a five-section tall stack with a flanged top. The crew stood on a platform with no support rails. This platform extended back from the last pair of wheels by about five feet. Two or three rods supported the tall stack. A second drawing purported to be the West Point shows a short, stubby boiler with a three-section medium-height stack. This has a platform extending only inches beyond the last pair of wheels and a substantial iron set of rails protects the crew from a fall. There are no rods to support the stack.

The West Point was the first locomotive to have an assigned tender. The first version was a conventional flatcar with a barrel of water and a pile of firewood to feed the fire. The West Point's actual tender came from West Point Foundry later in 1831. The water was carried in a large cask set sideways to the car and at the rear, while the wood was piled between the paneled wood sides of the car. A simple four-wheel tender, it represented the first step in supplying materials for a locomotive.

Nevertheless, the West Point did not go into regular service and remained in the shop to bring its performance up to the standard set by the Best Friend.

The West Point, the second locomotive of the Charleston & Hamburg, is shown about to depart from Line Street in Charleston. The side-tracked Best Friend of Charleston is already old-fashioned when compared to the new, sleek horizontal boiler of the West Point, which is making its maiden journey. Note the cotton bales on the barrier car. *Commissioned by American Cyanamid Co. for an advertising campaign. Author's collection.*

The West Point, second locomotive of the Charleston & Hamburg, is seen here in a contemporary artist's drawing illustrating the excursion of March 5, 1831, that shows the engineer and fireman standing on a platform lacking any safety railings. Built with a horizontal boiler, this locomotive was driven by a pair of pistons, mounted by the engineer, which drove the rear drivers using a pair of internal cranks on the driver's axle. The artist's representation seems to be cobbled together, as the two passenger cars at the end are to a different scale and even the track ties do not match. In fact, the passengers are exactly the same as those seen in the stockholders' train of January 15, 1831. *Author's collection.*

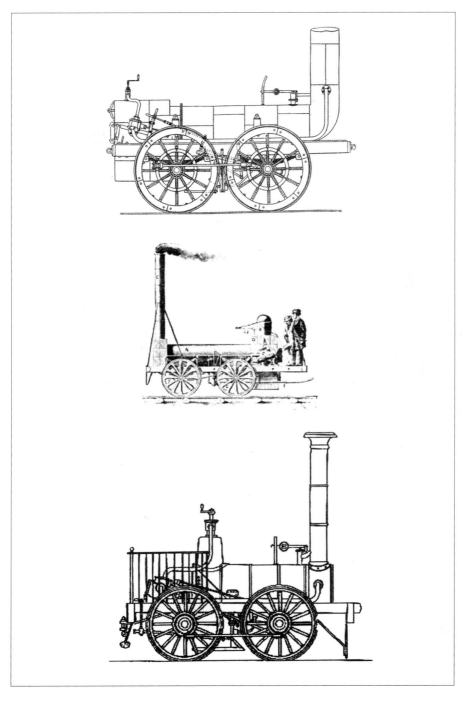

Drawings of the West Point differ in the details. One shows a rather plain horizontal boiler with a rotary hand crank to regulate the steam to the pistons and a smokestack that curves gently from the boiler to the stack. Another shows a steam dome at the engineer's end of the boiler but lacks the rotary crank and has a five-section smokestack that rises from a smoke box at the end of the boiler. A third shows a three-section smokestack rising from the boiler itself, a steam dome with the rotary hand crank and safety railings to protect the engineer. *Author's collection.*

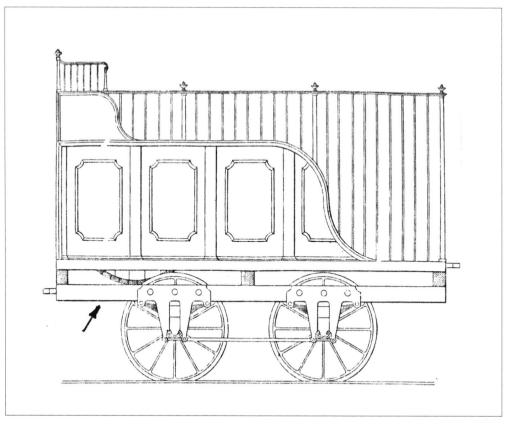

The West Point had a special tender built in April of 1831 by the West Point Foundry. Water was carried in a wooden barrel along with a fenced section for the fuel. Note that the car is sprung to ease any pounding on the rails. An original wash drawing is at the Engineering Societies Library in New York and was the source for this engineering drawing. *Author's collection.*

A Barrier Car

To reassure the passengers who had a not altogether unreasonable fear of a boiler explosion, the company began to run a barrier car, a small four-wheel flatcar piled high with six bales of cotton, between the locomotive and the passenger cars. But this precaution did not prevent a catastrophe that occurred as the Best Friend sat apart from its train on June 17, 1831.

Derailment at a Turnout

The final surveyed route to Hamlet was agreed upon on June 4, 1831. It was designed to be built with nine turnouts, or passing places, along the line. While common today, this was an innovation with a parallel track joined to the mainline by two switches, one at each end. These turnouts (or sidings) would allow two trains to run by each other at these locations with a depot agent to assist. In addition, twelve pumps or watering places were to be established to water the locomotives.

Horatio Allen wrote a report to Elias Horry, president of the C&HRR, on May 14, 1831, to explain a derailment accident that had occurred on May 13. Apparently an "ill-disposed person" had loosened the fastening at the turnout and left the "tongue, which guides the wheel through the turnout," in a "wide derangement." The person "who had management of the engine" had passed the turnout at an "imprudent speed" when the tongue "was probably shaken from its place by the speed with which the engine and one car preceeded" before the car that followed picked the point and toppled off the track, suffering some damage. It is likely that Nicholas Darrell was the engineer on this train.

Allen issued orders that all trains were to "pass the turnout at moderate speed" and "the attention of the person in charge to be constantly kept on the road in advance of the engine."

Best Friend Explodes

Nicholas Darrell and his fireman boarded the Best Friend on Friday morning, June 17, after getting orders to run up the line "to meet the lumber cars at the Forks of the Road" where Dorchester Road and State Road diverged. This was at or near Eight Mile House, where a turntable had been installed to turn the equipment. Arriving without incident, Darrell told his fireman to turn the locomotive while he checked the lumber cars. The locomotive was turned on the table and while still on the table, the fireman pressed down on the safety valve to end the constant loud hissing noise of escaping steam. Unfamiliar with the equipment or its purpose, the man finally found that if he held the valve down by sitting on it, the noise would stop. No one seemed to notice the silence until, with no means to release the ever building pressure in the boiler, the upright cylinder of iron that held the boiling water suddenly exploded at the bottom without warning, throwing the fireman through the air. Badly scalded and with his thigh broken, he died of his injuries a day or two later. A second black man received a severe cut in the face and a slight cut on his breast.

The boiler was thrown from the locomotive platform some twenty-five feet. Darrell, as the engineer of the train, had been nearby arranging the lumber cars so they were properly connected and ready to be drawn back to the city. He was suddenly shocked by the blast of steam as the boiler launched itself into the air. He was scalded from the shoulder blade down across his back.

Darrell wrote later, "When I ran the Best Friend, I had a Negro fireman to fire, clean and grease the machine. This Negro, annoyed at the noise occasioned by the blowing off the steam, fastened the valve-lever down and sat upon it which caused the explosion, badly injuring him, from the effects of which he died afterward, and scalding me." The death of the fireman was the first fatality on an American railroad and provided a sobering, pensive period in which the enthusiasm of the first six months was dampened.

Nicholas Darrell is stunned and then scalded by steam from the exploding Best Friend of Charleston as his fireman is blown from the machine, along with the boiler and smokestack. *Drawing by author.*

The explosion ended all train service on the Charleston & Hamburg for a full month, from June 17 until July 15, 1831, when the West Point was assigned into regular service. Darrell now became the engineer of the West Point locomotive.

Word of the explosion traveled rapidly across the East Coast, where other railroad experiments were underway. The Baltimore & Ohio, which offered a prize for the first working steam locomotive submitted for test that complied with a number of requirements, stipulated, "There must be two safety-valves, one of which must be completely out of the reach of the engine-man, and neither of which must be fastened down while the engine is working." This is obviously a direct reference to the loss of the Best Friend of Charleston. The B&O trials found only one engine, built by Phineas Davis, to meet the requirements and late in the summer of 1831, this Davis engine pulled four loaded cars weighing fourteen tons some thirteen miles in an hour. Considering the trial run of the West Point, six months earlier, on March 5, 1831, in which five loaded cars had been hauled five miles in eighteen minutes, the Charleston & Hamburg was far superior in its daily operations.

EQUIPMENT IN MID-1831

Darrell's preoccupation with assembling a train of lumber cars calls attention to the equipment in service at that time. Most of the freight equipment consisted of simple four-wheel flatcars that were adaptable to hauling bales of cotton, barrels of naval stores and other bulky goods. Lumber cars were specially adapted to haul long lengths of newly cut lumber back to Charleston, where it could be put to use or shipped out from the port of Charleston to Northern ports, Europe or the West Indies. The company had a limited number of flat roof passenger cars, at least six, designed to carry twenty passengers each, as well as a special events flatcar designed to carry a musical band. A barrier car loaded with six bales of cotton to shield the passengers from a boiler explosion was operated during these early months.

This drawing was a section of the West Point excursion of March 5, 1831, to illustrate the typical four-wheel car that served all purposes on the Charleston & Hamburg Rail Road. *Author's collection.*

THE UNITED STATES MAIL

The railroad became the first to carry the U.S. mail when the post office realized the tremendous advantage the trains had over any other carriage in the area. As early as November 30, 1831, the mail was carried from Line Street up the line to 12 Mile House, where it was transferred to mail stages. The Charleston paper reported this event on December 1 and reported that the round trip had taken two hours and ten minutes. In February of 1832, the mail for Augusta, Camden and Columbia was regularly carried twelve miles from Line Street to the transfer station, and this continued on a regular basis. The company reported in the Annual Report issued in May 1832 that they had taken in $483.34 from carrying the mail in the first five months.

TRACK EXPANSION FOR THE CHARLESTON & HAMBURG

Expansion of the line toward Hamburg was slow at first. In 1831, the track gang was able to lay about three quarters of a mile of track in a month, slowed by the swampy and marshy land that was being tamed. There were no conventional roads in the area and the survey essentially was a straight line across the Pine Barrens. By the end of the year, the Charleston & Hamburg was fifteen miles long and had reached the hamlet of Woodstock.

1832 – The Second Year of Operation

The loss of the Best Friend in 1831 after only six months of service was daunting, but the company knew it had to have a replacement locomotive as quickly as possible. SCC&RR again contracted with West Point Foundry, which came up with a dramatically different type of machine.

3. SOUTH CAROLINA (2-4-2)

The new 0-4-0 West Point had been put to work on a day-to-day basis in July of 1831 to replace the Best Friend. It remained the C&H's only locomotive until February of 1832, when the massive 2-4-2 South Carolina was put into service.

Horatio Allen had designed this new style of locomotive with eight driving wheels to gain greater pulling power. Allen had visited with John B. Jervis at his Albany, New York home in the summer of 1830 and 1831 and the men had discussed the merits of a leading truck to guide a locomotive into a curve. Jervis thought it best to have a leading four-wheel truck and rigid drivers to follow that were fixed to the frame of the locomotive. Allen wanted a two-truck locomotive with the drivers carried on a separate frame. This was to allow the wheels to flex as they worked through curves or switches or along uneven track. He finished drawings of this type of machine and gave it to the West Point Foundry in 1831, and the machine was shipped to Charleston for assembly. The $5,000 machine arrived from New York on January 15 and had to be assembled and tested. Allen recalled, "I took the position that no long road for general passenger and freight purposes could maintain itself without the use of eight-wheel locomotives and that probably ten-wheel locomotives would also be found desirable. It is of some interest that their introduction, without patent, was in a great degree the means of saving the railroad companies and the public from charges for their use."

This was the first articulated locomotive in the world. It was a machine that supported a pair of twin barrel boilers on each end extending from the single firebox in the middle over two wheel assemblies to distribute weight over the strap rail on wooden track. The boiler was, of necessity, a complex arrangement of piping, and this probably led to the early demise of the South Carolina. The engineer rode upon a platform built above the firebox of this 2-2+2-2 mechanical monster. While the machine proved to be far more powerful than either the Best Friend or the West Point, the locomotive was hard riding

The South Carolina was shown with a typical tender, and a train of four freight cars loaded with bales of cotton and protected by a canvas cover. However, the drawing is again cobbled together, as the ties beneath the South Carolina and tender do not match the ties beneath the freight cars. This suggests some artist's license was used to prepare some of the drawings. *Author's collection.*

A contemporary artist's drawing of the South Carolina, essentially two steam locomotives with an articulated connection. Each engine had two parallel boilers and a single piston mounted between them and below the smokestack driving an internal crank on the drivers. The engineer stood on a platform between the two sections of the locomotive. *Author's collection.*

and was known as a stiff machine that required care in approaching curves. However, it offered the advantage of not having to be turned at the end of the line.

Contemporary drawings show the engineer perched between the two boilers and above the firebox with a small railing for support. A short steam stack is behind the engineer and each boiler has a four-section tall stack.

Performance never was quite up to the expectation, but the South Carolina and others of its class lasted to 1838, when they were all withdrawn from service. Nevertheless, six, eight and ten drivered locomotives as well as articulated machines were used throughout the country in the early part of the twentieth century by every major railroad.

The year 1832 saw the Charleston & Hamburg put more resources into the track expansion to reach Hamburg. Some 1,317 men were at work building the trackwork in February of 1832. The company benefited from the donation of the right-of-way in many areas, as well as the permission to use the timber along the way to build the trestlework. However, the labor had to be purchased, and, in many cases, slaves from the local plantations were obtained for a set fee to build the railroad across the surveyed route.

The track gang reached Summerville in the summer of 1832. This was the first town of consequence to be reached on the route and it actually generated some freight headed back to Charleston. The trees were cut from this heavily forested area and converted to lumber, dried and shipped back down the line using special lumber freight cars.

On October 3, 1832, the company began to run two passenger-only through trains still farther up the line from Summerville. They ran from Line Street at 6:00 a.m. and 1:00 p.m. up to Ridge Road, located between Cypress Swamp and Four Hole Swamp. The trains returned at 9:00 a.m. and 3:00 p.m. While at first the idea of running a train twice a day to a road crossing in a desolate swamp area seems ludicrous, the farmers and settlers in the area were treated to first-rate service that allowed them to go to Charleston and return in the same day, which had previously been impossible.

Just a little more than a month later, the track gang reached the hamlet of Branchville on November 7, 1832. Branchville had been named for a meeting held under the branches of a large tree back during the Revolutionary War. (Some sources have said the name derived from a later railroad branch line that was built to Columbia, but this is not so.)

By the end of the year, some forty-five miles had been put in place and the railroad was now sixty miles long. The rails had reached the east bank of the Edisto River, nearly halfway to Hamburg.

Train Wreck at Bee's Farm

The C&H was the scene of the first passenger train wreck in the United States, an unenviable first. This accident occurred on Thursday, April 19, 1832. A party of war veterans, the Northern Volunteers under the command of Captain Egelston and their guests, had traveled up the tracks of the C&H to the farm of Bernard Bee to celebrate the anniversary of the Battle of Lexington that had set off the Revolutionary War. After the festivities, the party returned to the three-car train that was pulled by the West Point. The *Charleston Courier* reported what happened next.

> *They had just entered the cars and started on their return to town when, after proceeding a few hundred yards, the hind axel of the forward car suddenly gave way and the car, which was an open one, striking with much violence on the framework of the road, before the locomotive could be stopped, was torn in pieces and the passengers, upwards of thirty in number, precipitated into a low swampy place filled with mud and water, over which the road passed. Four or five of the number, we regret to state, were very seriously injured. Those most seriously hurt were taken back to the house where they received all possible attention until the day following when they were conveyed to town upon the railroad and we are happy to state all are now considered to be out of danger.*

Horatio Allen, as chief engineer, investigated the circumstances and reported that the "brittle quality" of the wrought-iron axles together with the overweight on the car, which was designed to carry only twenty passengers, had caused the mishap. Shortly thereafter the axles of these cars were converted from $2\frac{1}{4}$ to $2\frac{3}{4}$ inches to increase their strength.

Allen had the wheels changed to wrought iron on a common axle with bearings on both sides of the wheel. He also redesigned the passenger cars to be suspended below the wheel axle so that the car body would be only six inches from the rail top. This was to provide a limited fall of the car if either the wheel or axle were to fail. No more than twenty passengers were to be carried in any one car.

1A. PHOENIX (0-4-0)

The West Point and the South Carolina were used from February 24 to October 18, 1832, to haul the scheduled trains. The remains of the Best Friend had been returned to Thomas Dotterer's shop and a new locomotive was rebuilt. In place of the wood wheels with iron tires and crank axles, the rebuilt machine had cast-iron wheels with wrought-iron tires and straight axles. This was the first locomotive ever built with outside connections and straight axles, although the Native, a Dotterer locomotive built in 1833, also incorrectly claimed this first use. A new small vertical boiler was installed and the locomotive was placed back in service as the Phoenix under Henry Raworth as the new engineer.

There were four engineers on the line by this time: Nicholas Darrell, Henry Raworth, John Eason and Julius Petsch.

THE SOUTH CAROLINA EXPLODES

The three locomotives were used until December 27, 1832, when the South Carolina's boiler exploded and it was sent to the shops. The West Point and the Phoenix were pressed into maintaining the train service from December 27 to April 10.

The Phoenix, rebuilt with parts from the Best Friend of Charleston, has the rotary steam control valve, a safety railing for the engineer, connected drivers and an attached tender area. *Author's collection*.

The South Carolina remained out of service until April 10 of the next year. A number of design problems became evident when it returned to service. Only a few weeks later, it was again taken out of service and new frames had to be designed and built to provide better support for the barrel boilers. The original design had led to repeated breakage of the steam pipes, as the frames were not stable. The redesigned new frame alleviated this problem completely. The machines axles were also found to be too brittle and they broke several times before this redesign of 1833 and substitution of a more substantial iron material.

1833 – The Longest Railroad
in the World

1833 was to prove to be a banner year as the Charleston & Hamburg Rail Road finally reached the warehouses at Hamburg on the Savannah River. The final push was not easy as we shall see. Finding a way to descend from the high ridge at Aiken down to the creek bed below was a major challenge for the line.

MIDWAY, SOUTH CAROLINA

By February 7, 1833, the tracks of the C&H had been extended much farther and had crossed the Edisto River and reached a location named Midway, as it was half the distance to Hamburg. Operations over this sixty-five-mile route with only the two small 0-4-0 locomotives made scheduling difficult, and it was soon clear that the line needed another engine like the South Carolina, as the freight trains were becoming longer and heavier.

3A. CONSTITUTION (2-4-2)

The rebuilt and redesigned South Carolina emerged from the Eason & Dotterer shops as the new Constitution and returned to service on the Charleston & Hamburg Rail Road on April 19. The three locomotives—Phoenix, West Point and Constitution—then operated together until June 4, when the Barnwell went into service.

4. CHARLESTON (2-4-2)

In March of 1833, the new Charleston, a sister of the South Carolina, arrived in Charleston from the West Point Foundry for assembly. But the work on this locomotive went slowly and had not been completed when a second locomotive (the Barnwell) in parts arrived from New York. The boiler of the Charleston was found to be poorly constructed and had to be rebuilt. The smokestack and discharge pipes were redesigned by West Point, and this design proved to be difficult to control the draught. The company replaced the stack with one as originally designed and the draught problem was eliminated. The frames and axles were rebuilt to follow the example of the South Carolina. The machine then went into service on September 1, 1833, as the Charleston. The strength of the valve gearing was soon found to be inadequate and it was replaced about December 1833.

5. BARNWELL (2-4-2)

The newly assembled Barnwell, the third engine of the South Carolina class, was pressed into service immediately on June 4 and the West Point was then withdrawn from service for heavy maintenance. The valve gearing on the Barnwell was stronger than the two previous locomotives of this class; however, it was still troublesome. The water pumps on this machine did not work as well, and they were particularly fouled when brackish water was siphoned from nearby streams. This led to low water in the boiler and the flue piping was impaired by the excessive heat because of the low water level.

The Phoenix, Constitution and Barnwell served the C&H until September 1, 1833, when the Charleston entered service and the Constitution was withdrawn for new side frames and additional boiler alterations. The Barnwell was removed from service on September 20, 1833, to have new flues installed. However, it remained out of service beyond November 1833.

6. EDISTO (2-4-2)

These three locomotives, Phoenix, Charleston and Barnwell, were then joined by the Edisto, a fourth engine in the South Carolina class, on September 11, 1833. This was the first time that four locomotives were simultaneously on the line.

The Edisto had the best valve gearing of any of the earlier locomotives. However, one of the wheels broke at the hub along with two of the side legs that supported the boilers. It was apparent that some extraordinary strain had occurred, as the other similar wheels had not failed in service. Allen set out to determine what had caused the wreck.

Ten days later, the Barnwell was taken out of service. The company was by this time only too aware that the oversize South Carolina–class locomotives were plagued with trouble due to unsound workmanship and inadequate engineering in proportioning the working valve gear to the strain of daily operation.

The Edisto was the last of the class to be ordered, and in fact, no other railroad built a similar double-ended locomotive until thirty-three years later, when the Festiniog Railway in Wales experimented with the design in 1866.

EQUIPMENT IN 1833

The West Point was taken out of service in June of 1833 and given a new frame and new wheels with stronger axles. However, the parts were slow in being constructed

Purported to show the first use of a headlamp, this drawing shows the Best Friend of Charleston (which blew up in 1831) pushing the two flatcars, one with a wood fire in a cage on a bed of sand and the other used as a spacer. However, the reflector mentioned in contemporary reports is not illustrated here. This is a twentieth-century illustration mixing an 1831 locomotive with an 1833 headlamp based on limited information. *Author's collection.*

and the locomotive was still in the shop in November waiting for the final parts and reassembly.

At this time the line had placed in service the 2-4-2 Barnwell and the 2-4-2 Edisto, which, with the West Point, Constitution, Phoenix and Charleston, totaled six locomotives.

In addition to the locomotives listed above, the company had built fifty-six freight cars, nearly all the basic flatcar design; eleven lumber cars that were longer flats designed to carry longer loads; fourteen tenders that were assigned to locomotives as needed; and eight passenger cars that were the same basic flatcar with a door in the side for entering and exiting.

In the annual report, the company reported that broken axles were the principal cause of accidents on the road. Allen set out to find a solution for this persistent problem.

When the Charleston & Hamburg decided to try night operations to reduce the heavy amount of traffic during the day, authorities quickly found that they needed a way to light the track ahead for safety. Two small flatcars were assigned to provide a headlight. The first car had a bed of sand on the flat boards and a fire of pine knots made a bright light. The second car held a sheet iron reflector to project the light forward and up the track. This is thought to be the first attempt at lighting the right-of-way for night operations.

An alternative report from September of 1833 exists in which the C&H reported it owned seven locomotives (see the Native below), as well as forty-six cars, slaves worth $6,146 and real estate valued at $15,388.25.

The fare for travel on the trains was set to be low and affordable. On the run to Summerville, the train stopped at Jerioco, 8.5 miles for 25 cents; Sineath's, 12 miles for

37.5 cents; Woodstock, 14.5 miles for 50 cents; Ladson's Road, 17 miles for 62.5 cents; and Summerville, 22 miles for 75 cents. Clergymen on duty could ride free and children under twelve as well as servants traveling with their owners could ride for half fare. Free persons of color had to pay full fare. The local paper pointed out that a bale of cotton could travel from Midway, much farther up the line, for only 50 cents.

THE AIKEN PLANES

The remaining sixty miles to Hamburg were laid in the first eight months of 1833 at the rate of seven and a half miles per month. But one roadblock of significance remained to be conquered at Aiken, South Carolina: a descent to the river valley below the bluff town.

The town of Aiken, named for President Aiken of the C&H who had died in 1831, was 510 feet above sea level, but the gradient from Charleston to Aiken was negligible. Not so the grade from Aiken down to Hamburg, at 360 feet above sea level. The C&H felt that direct descent via inclined planes was preferred to a roundabout descent over a much greater distance. The inclined planes, as installed, were built with three grades of descent, the steepest being one in twelve. The planes were double tracked and operated by gravity. One car would descend while attached to a cable, which in turn was fastened to an unloaded and lighter ascending car. Black workers were later used to raise or lower the cars by a hand-cranked winch. Still later, the company installed two thirty-five-horsepower steam engines to raise and lower the cars.

While this may seem an awkward solution, it was the foremost theory at the time for crossing mountains. The Ashley Planes near Wilkes-Barre, Pennsylvania, operated into the mid-twentieth century for the New Jersey Central, and the Mahoning Planes near Tamaqua, Pennsylvania, operated for the Reading Railroad at the same time. In both cases, the roundabout continuous track route was later found to be superior, and these planes were abandoned by 1860.

The Aiken Planes are today seen as the median of Park Street and some of the bridle paths in Hitchcock Woods, southwest of the city. The intersection of Laurens and Park Streets is northeast of the original plane.

The C&H tracks then followed a small stream from the foot of the inclines to Hamburg. Hamburg had been started as a planned community by an individual who sought to take the freight trade from Augusta. In later years, Hamburg gained prominence as a local center of the slave trade, which was banned in Georgia. Georgians, however, were free to cross the river at Augusta and buy or sell at the Hamburg market.

THE LONGEST RAILROAD IN THE WORLD

The tracks finally reached Hamburg, South Carolina, a long 136 miles from Charleston, on October 2, 1833. The Charleston & Hamburg, as a consequence, became the longest

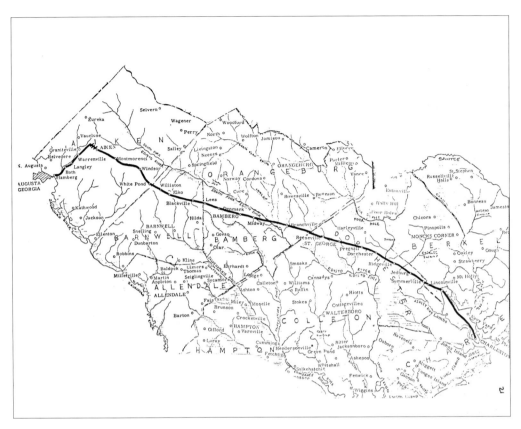

The completed route of the Charleston & Hamburg Rail Road is seen here. Note that the western half of the line ran on a ridge between the South Edisto River watershed on the north, and the tributaries of other rivers on the south. *Map by author.*

railroad in the world at that time. The cost assigned to the project for building the track was $950,000, which came close to meeting the original estimate. Henry Schultz of Hamburg donated land for the "depository" at the end of the line. This was at Covington and Tilman Streets. (Depository is clearly the origin of the railroad "depot," used on nearly all of the lines built in the United States.)

The construction had been slow because of delays in trestle building, especially in areas of quicksand and in crossing over "hardpan," which could not easily be worked with the tools of that day. In addition, the expense of constructing inclined planes near Aiken to lower the railway equipment one at a time to the flood plain of the Savannah River had delayed the final construction phase.

The primary financial goal of the Charleston & Hamburg was to begin to move at least half of the 170,000 bales of cotton that arrived at the Augusta and Hamburg market each year. This would give the line some 85,000 bales that each weighed 320 pounds, or 13,000 tons of prime cotton bound for Charleston, a commodity that had never arrived at the port city in volume. There was approximately the same freight weight expected to travel inland from Charleston to Hamlet, which would provide the new railroad with some $250,000 worth of freight each year. Passenger business was estimated to be one hundred passengers a day going the entire length of the line, which would add an additional $203,000 per year to the income. Overall then, the Charleston & Hamburg was poised to become a cash cow, providing $453,000 a year.

Elias Horry, president of the C&H between 1831 and 1834, spoke at the Medical College in Charleston on October 2, 1833. His speech, "An address Respecting the Charleston & Hamburg Rail Road and on the Rail Road System as Regards a Large Portion of the Southern and Western States of the North American Union," is additional confirmation that the railroad was popularly known as the C&H. In this speech, Horry referred to a railroad convention held at Asheville, North Carolina, a few weeks earlier, in which a new line out of Tennessee and the North had been proposed. "The Asheville Convention has fixed its point of destination to be Columbia [South Carolina] and thence it will be extended to our Charleston & Hamburg Rail Road." This proposed line was stillborn, yet within the decade the line from the C&HRR to Columbia had been built and began operating.

The next day, October 3, the line opened to Hamburg and a special train was run from Charleston to Aiken with the governor of South Carolina and his entourage. At Aiken, they disembarked and the party continued to Hamburg on handcars, since the steam locomotive for shuttling cars from Hamburg to the bottom of the Aiken planes had not yet arrived in Charleston on the *America*.

The Charleston & Hamburg Rail Road was commemorated on July 7, 1970, at Hamburg by the United States as a National Historic Civil Engineering Landmark. A plaque dedicating the line was unveiled at the Hamburg railroad station. (The plaque actually reads South Carolina Canal & Railroad Company.)

COMMUNITIES

Although at the time the C&H was built there were very few communities along the right-of-way, the route soon was lined with hamlets and county seats. From Charleston the line passed through Summerville, Ridgeville, Pregnall, Saint George, Reevesville, Branchville, Midway, Bamberg, Denmark, Blackville, Williston, White Pond, Windsor, Montmorency and Aiken before reaching the inclined planes. The line then passed through Warrenville and Bath to terminate at Hamburg across from Augusta.

A RIDE ON THE CHARLESTON & HAMBURG

A traveler from New England rode from Charleston to Hamburg during the first months of operation and reported his adventure in the *St. Augustine (FL) Herald*. The "line was single track with turnouts at various places. The rails of the track are built of the timber of the country, hard pine full of pitch." The train would go "as if Satan were at its heels, now it scarcely dragged its freight." Several times it came to a dead stand for "want of steam." Low ground and the swamps areas were crossed in places as high as fifty feet above the water level.

The traveler arrived in Blackville (named for Alexander Black, who had first chartered the line) in the afternoon. "Two or three log house and one half built 'tavern' amid a half burnt forest of pitch pine" described the town. Here he spent the night, having made ninety miles from 8:30 in the morning to 6:30 at night. The "tavern" had five "rooms," each part of a row of stalls with partitions between each. Thirty passengers shared the accommodations of the five rooms. With dinner described as "miserable—the cooking probably that of slaves," breakfast ("I make no complaint except of its cooking") and the use of the room, the bill came to four dollars. It is entirely possible that the food was well prepared but unfamiliar to the palate of a New England Yankee.

The country became hilly soon after passing from Blackville and at Aiken the passengers and baggage were transferred to a new car to go down the inclined plane. The train upon which they had arrived was dispatched back to Charleston.

The car on the inclined plane was lowered by two black workers on either side of the track who turned a crank with a cable attached to the car. The plane was 3,800 feet in length and descended 150 feet. (No mention of three planes was made.)

7. NATIVE

This locomotive was considered a native, as it came directly from the shops of Eason & Dotterer in Charleston. Thomas Dotterer had been active in "mechanical science" since 1815, when he operated a shop known as Johnson & Dotterer at Gadsden's Wharf in Charleston. By 1819, the shop was moved to the foot of Hasell Street on the Cooper River and in association with Robert Eason, it was known as Eason & Dotterer. This shop had set up the Best Friend of Charleston and the other locomotives that had been sent by ship from the West Point Foundry in New York.

In 1833, the C&H contracted with Eason & Dotterer to design and build a locomotive not to exceed six tons in weight. Dotterer introduced the first use of the outside connection on this locomotive, which was "condemned by some on the ground that it was impracticable, and would injure the superstructure of the road by the constant shaking it would cause."

The trial trip of the Native was revealing and surprising. The *Charleston Daily Courier* reported, "After steam was raised, the engineer was directed to run up the road until he met the down train and then return to the city. The day passed and night came on, but nothing was heard of the little Native." Many were the discouraging predictions made by those who were wedded to the belief that Charleston mechanics could not build a locomotive. Some went so far as to abuse the builders by saying that the "confounded little thing had broken down and obstructed the road, thus delaying the arrival of the incoming train." Their surprise, however, was great when at a later hour in the night, the little Native came puffing down the road drawing the whole train including the great locomotive.

It soon became clear that the Native had proceeded on down line much farther than expected until it came upon the "down train," which had become disabled. The Native was thus given "an opportunity to test her powers fully. Her arrival was announced with long and loud cheers and many were the praises bestowed upon the enterprising builders."

James Eason recalled the event in greater detail.

> *The locomotive did not arrive with the train. Great uneasiness was manifested by the officers of the company, for in those days everybody interested attended at the arrival of a locomotive. Finally night came on; neither the regular train nor the little Native was in sight, and the murmurings could be heard in knots of persons and officials that the damned thing had broken the road or blown up or some other casualty had happened to her and prevented the arrival of the other locomotive and train.*
>
> *Imagine Mr. Dotterer's feelings; but behold him, the man of genius, standing amid the bickering of men, almost fearing that his little engine was the cause of the delay, when a voice cried out, "She's coming!" and the sparks from the smoke pipe were observed. Then a general rush to hear the news, to see what caused the detention, and learn the fate of the poor home-made Native pulling locomotive and train, when a cry from a faithful friend of Mr. Dotterer, "Why, 'tis the Native pulling locomotive and train!"*
>
> *Then look at Thomas Dotterer, with a heart full, with teardrops on his eyes, as the smile of successful championship and confidence in his work played upon his countenance. I stood beside him at that moment and share with him in his pride.*

The local company eventually supplied seven locomotives to the C&H over a five-year period.

8. HAMBURG (0-4-0)

The West Point Foundry provided another 0-4-0 model to the Charleston & Hamburg in 1833. This locomotive was built to an English plan used to build a Camden & Amboy locomotive for service between Camden, New Jersey (across the Delaware River from Philadelphia), and Amboy, New Jersey (across the Hudson River from New York). Again, shipped by sea to Charleston, the locomotive arrived in October 1833. The machine was assembled by Eason & Dotterer and emerged as the Hamburg. However, the axles proved to be weak and failed in the first three test runs. By design, the Hamburg was expected to be one-third more powerful than the eight-wheel class of engines.

THE GREAT TRAIN FIRE

Five days after through service to Hamburg was initiated, the Charleston & Hamburg sent a train toward Charleston that had an unfortunate experience. It was October 8,

1833, which was a day the line was not soon to forget. The train was composed of a locomotive, five freight cars and two passenger cars trailing behind. It was somewhere northwest of Summerville when a freight car was found to have caught fire from the sparks sent skyward from the locomotive's stack. This fire was extinguished by the crew using water from the swamp and the train began to roll again.

The freight cars were heavily laden with bales of cotton that were protected against fire by heavy canvas covers, but the ends of the bales became exposed as the train picked up speed and the canvas flapped in the wind. Only a mile down the line, one of the passenger cars began to flame and the crew, alerted by the shouts of the passengers, once more put out the fire with swamp water near the tracks. However, when the train was only five miles out from Summerville, the passengers cried out yet again that the last freight car was on fire. The crew stopped the train, but could find no water at this location. Rather than risk the loss of the passenger cars or harm to the riders, the freight cars were uncoupled and the locomotive and the five freight cars proceeded several yards down the track. Here the burning car, by now burning out of control, was uncoupled and the engine and four remaining freight cars moved still farther down the track. The burning car held twenty-one bales of cotton, which were totally consumed, together with the freight car and the wooden rails where the car stood.

When the fire was out, the crew tossed the debris to the side, tied a rope from the last freight car to the passenger cars and pulled the two cars over the burned rails. With the train re-coupled, it proceeded to Charleston and arrived three hours late with the passengers full of tales of adventure.

FREIGHT RATES

Rates for freight were set at half of those charged for stages and freight wagons. This was so economical that raftsmen, who directly competed by rafting cotton and freight down the Edisto River from Orangeburg, would now send their paddling boats back to the Edisto near Orangeburg by train from Charleston.

COMPETITION: THE CENTRAL OF GEORGIA RAILROAD AND CANAL COMPANY

The success of the Charleston & Hamburg was a shock to the city fathers in Savannah. In the first two months of operation, the freight coming down the Savannah River began to diminish. On December 20, 1833, a new railroad was chartered as the Central of Georgia Railroad & Canal Company (CofGA RR&CC). Savannah backed the line while it sent teams of surveyors out to plot a route to Macon, Georgia, in 1834.

The public knowledge that the C&HRR had cost $5,600 per mile was daunting to the banks of the area, and interest began to falter. The company then applied for an amended charter to permit it to carry out a banking business and was reorganized in

January of 1836 as the Central Railroad & Banking Company of Georgia. With the backing of its own bank, the line began to grade the accepted route in the fall of 1836, and the first twenty-six miles were opened for operation in May of 1838.

COMPETITION: THE GEORGIA RAIL ROAD

The Georgia Rail Road was chartered on December 21, 1833, to build a line from Augusta northwest toward Chattanooga. Surveys were started in June of 1835, but the company could not raise funds for construction.

   A revised charter was granted in December of 1835 that permitted the reorganization of the company as the Georgia Railroad & Banking Company, a move duplicated by the CofGA RR&CC only a month later. The first ten miles of the line were opened in January of 1837. This line was looked on with interest, as it offered a potential cooperative route to the northwest corner of Georgia.

1834 – Building a Fleet of Locomotives

The arrival of 1834, three months after the road through to Hamburg was opened, brought the sudden realization that the line was severely underpowered, based on the tremendous increase in freight brought to the Hamburg depot for shipment. While a few locomotives were already ordered, it was imperative for the company to obtain a large number of machines very quickly. Aware that the small West Point Foundry would be unable to supply the number needed, the Charleston & Hamburg turned to Mathias Baldwin, a new locomotive builder in Philadelphia, and to several British manufacturers. But there were a number of other critically important events that transpired early in the year.

The End of the Wooden Pile Roadbed

Early in 1834, the company discovered a very serious problem with the original wood pilings that supported the tracks through the swamp areas. The wood was rotting at the ground line, endangering the ability of the structure to support the heavy freight trains and the fast moving passenger trains. The company quickly began to replace the pilings with dirt embankments that could be dumped with the track in place and provided limited delays to the scheduled trains. In addition, the strap rail on wood that had been the original trackage was totally replaced with L-shaped iron flange that provided protection for the side of the wooden rails. The new flange strap was also designed to keep the locomotives and cars from beating the rail and subjecting it to extreme strain, since none of the railroad equipment was sprung. Allen had the equipment re-engineered to include springs to smooth out the pounding on the rails.

While the cost of the replacement was $463,132, nearly a half million dollars, the ever-increasing business provided no alternative solution. The new roadbed was nearly completed by the end of the year.

Entering the City of Charleston

The C&H had not been permitted to enter the city of Charleston when the line began construction in 1830. However, in March of 1834, with the approval of the city council, the line was extended from Line Street (the city limits) to Hudson Street and a new depot was built at Mary Street, between Meeting and King Streets.

WESTWARD CONNECTION

The Georgia Rail Road was built west from Augusta in 1834 through Athens to Decatur, Georgia, today a suburb of Atlanta. The company clearly had borrowed a page from the South Carolina line by building from a remote rural area in northwestern Georgia to Augusta, where farm products and other goods could be reshipped by steamboat to Savannah.

There appears to have been little or no interest in shipping Georgia goods over the Charleston & Hamburg to Charleston. However, the Georgia Rail Road Company soon realized that despite its contribution to the overall trip, it got a smaller, disproportionate part of the transportation money, and the transit of the goods slowed considerably over the steamboat portion of the trip.

No direct rail connection was provided between the two railroads other than wagons down the streets and transit by ferry from Augusta to Hamburg. The lobbying of the local teamsters to continue this procedure was successful for several years. This severely limited the through transportation of goods from Charleston to Decatur or back.

9. THE E.L. MILLER (4-2-0)

In Philadelphia, Mathias Baldwin, who was to become founder of the Baldwin Locomotive Works, had earlier designed a stationary steam engine for manufacturing, a small miniature locomotive for the Philadelphia Museum in 1831 and the full-size Old Ironsides for the Philadelphia, Germantown and Norristown Railroad Company's first run on November 23, 1832. Early in 1833, E.L. Miller, of Charleston ordered Baldwin's second full-size locomotive (and the first to utilize Baldwin's patented "half crank," in which the wheel formed an arm of the driving crank by use of an offset extension of the axle fastened to a wheel spoke). This locomotive, the C&H's ninth, was named for Miller and was completed on February 18, 1834.

The E.L. Miller was the first C&H locomotive to have a swiveling four-wheel truck at the front and a pair of fifty-four-inch driving wheels with the half crank located behind the firebox. The drivers were cast of solid bell metal, but these brass wheels, which were claimed to have superior adhesion, soon wore out. No other locomotives were built with the same feature, although some were built later with brass tires. The C&H was disappointed with the performance of the locomotive and did not order another Baldwin product until 1836, when its twenty-eighth engine, the Philadelphia, was ordered.

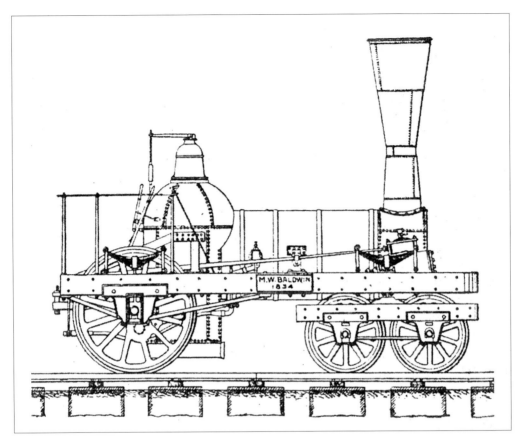

The second locomotive built by Mathias Baldwin was commissioned for the Charleston & Hamburg Rail Road in 1834, but the company was less than pleased with the machine and did not order from Baldwin again until three years later. *Author's collection.*

ENGLISH LOCOMOTIVES

The company hastened to order six English steam locomotives from three experienced builders. E. Bury Company of Liverpool built two 0-4-0 machines in 1834. Fenton of Leeds, England, built a 2-2-0 and Stevenson built three 0-4-0 machines. They are listed here. It may be that some of the locomotives were already built or partially built, as several arrived in Charleston by sea by midyear.

10.	Augusta	(0-4-0)	E. Bury
11.	Georgia	(0-4-0)	E. Bury
12.	Columbia	(2-2-0)	Fenton
13.	William Aiken	(0-4-0)	Stevenson #87
14.	E. Horry	(0-4-0)	Stevenson #99
15.	Edgefield	(0-4-0)	Stevenson

This engraving used on a South Carolina Rail Road one-dollar bill issued in Charleston seems to show the E.L. Miller, the second Baldwin locomotive to be built. It is the passenger car that draws our attention, as it is much longer than the original cars and seems to have paired windows that can drop into the side wall as desired. There is an open vestibule for boarding and apparently a center aisle between pairs of seats. While somewhat fanciful in the scenery, it seems to be accurate in the depiction of the equipment. *Author's collection.*

DAILY ROSTER ASSIGNMENTS

Daily operations in mid-1834 utilized the nine American engines. The C&H's three newest machines were received that year from the English Stevenson firm. These were assigned to haul the fast mixed trains from Charleston to Aiken. A typical train hauled four passenger cars and a baggage car, plus an assigned extra load. The 0-4-0 William Aiken regularly had one extra freight car assigned; the E. Horry hauled two additional freight cars; and the Edgefield was assigned four extra freight cars plus an additional baggage car for a total of ten cars in its trains.

The older locomotives were soon relegated as freight engines that could pull up to twenty-five freight cars. The 0-4-0 Hamburg and the 2-4-2 Charleston built by West Point; the 4-2-0 E.L. Miller built by Baldwin; and the locally built Native held this assignment. The remaining two locomotives were repositioned at the foot of the

Aiken planes and assigned to run from Hamburg to the base of the inclined planes. The small Phoenix hauled the passenger cars, while the massive 2-4-2 Edisto pulled the heavily laden freight cars from the cotton warehouses at Hamburg to the base of the planes. Here the cars were fairly rapidly hoisted to the top of the plane in Aiken, made up into the appropriate trains based on the locomotives available and dispatched to Charleston.

Pine Replaces Hardwood and Coke as the Fuel

The locomotives as built were designed to burn coke or hardwood. Horatio Allen redesigned the fireboxes to accept "pitch filled fat pine," which grew all along the track route. This redesign allowed crews that ran short on fuel to use scrap timber that lay along the rail route.

The engines normally operated at twenty-one miles per hour with six cars carrying fifty passengers and several freight cars. With a string of empties, they could roll along at forty miles per hour.

Experimental Freight Cars

Cotton bales overloaded the ability of the little freight cars' axles to withstand the constant pounding from the rail joints and switches. The company reported that broken axles were the most common cause of accidents on the road. Some of this obviously was from overloading the small two axle cars.

The standard freight car for the Charleston & Hamburg was a twelve-foot-long, four-wheel flatcar provided with a canvas cover to protect the bales. The standard bale of cotton weighed 320 pounds, a formidable weight. One of the standard freight cars could be loaded with 13 bales of cotton (a little more than two tons) and large shipments were, by necessity, placed on a large number of cars with the trains limited by locomotive power to pulling no more than fourteen cars (a little more than 29 tons). Shipments in excess of this 182-bale limit had to be carried on two trains or more.

About 1834, the company had two experimental freight cars built. The first was thirty feet long with two freight trucks of four wheels each, a design still in use on American railroads today. After the first trip, this thirty-foot car went into regular service on the line and carried a maximum load of sixty bales, but the company settled on fifty bales as the best load for the car.

The second car was forty feet long with two six-wheel freight trucks. This car made its first trip several weeks later and "passed the curves and the inclined plane with ease." It was clear to the company that the future belonged to the larger freight cars, since fewer cars could handle greater loads. Both of the cars in the test were nine feet wide and had tinplated iron sides, doors and roof. They were the first boxcars and were likely painted an economical red-lead color.

LONGEST AND HEAVIEST FREIGHT TRAIN

There were 149 freight cars in service in 1834, according to the Annual Report, and 99 of these were classed as "high covered" cars. This term may refer to the enclosed boxcars tested earlier in the year.

With several of the new heavy-duty boxcars in tow, the company experimented with a larger train pulled by three locomotives on December 13, 1834. This special freight pulled sixty cars carrying 986 bales of cotton. This 158-ton payload was claimed by the Charleston & Hamburg to be the longest and heaviest train operated on any American railway up to this time. Since the norm had been 29 tons pulled by one locomotive, the three locomotives would seem to have been limited to 87 tons, making this train nearly twice (1.8) as efficient as expected. This boiled down to the discovery that the larger cars allowed the line to haul more bales more efficiently with half the required locomotives, thus providing a huge profit margin.

ANIMAL PILOT

The C&H was unable to prevent maiming and death of many domestic animals, as well as wild animals, that wandered onto the unfenced right-of-way. The state, to prevent this toll, passed a law requiring the C&H to keep a man on the front of the engine to clear the track of animals. Cleverly, the railroad followed the spirit of the law, if not the directive, and mounted an iron model of a black boy with a flag in his hand as the engine's "pilot."

FINANCIAL DATA

The line had been financed through public subscription, of which Charleston bought 3,501 shares and the State of South Carolina purchased $250,000 in stock. This imbalance was to reposition the Charleston & Hamburg as a state-owned railroad, and no longer under the control of the Charleston men who initially financed the line. The overall cost of the line was assessed at $5,625 per mile.

The line carried 26,649 passengers in 1834; 34,283 in 1835; 39,216 in 1836; 41,554 in 1837; and 44,487 in 1838. The patronage slowed in 1839, with a mere 37,283 passengers buying tickets. Passengers in this tally might have ridden between Charleston and Ten Mile Station, or Summerville to Ladson, and Charleston to Hamburg passage was quite a bit less.

The C&H earned $58 a day when it began freight service in 1831. This figure climbed to $120 a day by the spring of 1833 and to $1,000 a day by 1835. Part of this increase in revenue was no doubt due to the completion of the 135-mile-long line through to Hamburg. Initially scheduled for twelve hours from start to finish, the C&H soon boasted of an eight-hour schedule.

HORATIO ALLEN RETURNS NORTH

Allen married Mary M. Simons in Charleston and left the city in 1835 to travel abroad to visit the capitals of Europe. Allen's contribution to the C&HRR was above and beyond what any of the Charleston financiers and merchants had expected when they hired the young man from New York.

Without his cleverness and ability to adapt to a continuous stream of change that occurred in the first three years of the C&HRR, the company would have failed and the revival of Charleston's fortunes would have been stifled.

The Possibility of Route Expansion

The success of the Charleston & Hamburg was clearly evident to everyone in the state, as well as in the industrialized areas along the East Coast. Entrepreneurs quickly began to copy the investment by establishing several railroad companies in the North, particularly in the Philadelphia area. But expansion of the Charleston & Hamburg line, or possibly the extension of the line by a second company, soon had the attention of the businessmen in Columbia, the state capital, who saw the potential of direct train service to and from Charleston.

COLUMBIA RAILROAD COMPANY (1833–1835)

The Columbia Railroad Company was chartered in December of 1833 to build a railroad line from Columbia to the mainline of the Charleston & Hamburg Rail Road. The route of the new railroad was first proposed to leave the rails of the C&H at Branchville and proceed through Orangeburg directly to Columbia, utilizing several inclined planes similar to the three near Aiken on the C&HRR. An incline of 190 feet would be required on the banks of the Congaree River and the river itself was to be crossed on a new second story of the existing wagon bridge.

An extension of the line to cross the Blue Ridge Mountains could run from Columbia up along the ridge through Newberry and Laurens to Greenville and then run on either of two routes, on which the track would either climb 1,102 feet over a distance of 18½ miles or follow Reedy Patch Creek and climb 1,344 feet in 11 miles. While interesting, this extension was not as important as laying track between Columbia and the Charleston & Hamburg.

This survey was reported in September of 1834. The road was found to be "indisputably necessary, not merely to the prosperity of Columbia, but to save it from decay and ruin."

But, financially unable to meet the terms of the charter, the company was disbanded in 1835. The Columbia Railroad Company was also informally referred to as the Columbia & Branchville Rail Road at this time, but this was never a legally recognized name.

1835—Freight Rates

As the Charleston & Hamburg first established freight rates, the cost for shipments was based on the mileage between the depots. The published rate was given in a table based on the distance from Charleston, with the greatest rate set for Hamburg. In addition, the company had a price differential between heavy and light loads. For example, a cubic foot of light goods shipped from Hamburg to Charleston was carried for only fourteen cents. Heavy materials were charged by the hundred-weight. A single hundred-weight carried between Hamburg and Charleston was priced at fifty cents. However, the price provided some additional benefits as the freight bill provided for one week's storage at the terminal and, in addition, full fire insurance for the material at no additional coast.

In the meantime, the Charleston & Hamburg needed still more motive power and again went to two English firms with good reputations: Vulcan Foundry and Stevenson & Tayleur Company. The new machines copied the 4-2-0 wheel arrangement of the E.L. Miller locomotive from Mathias Baldwin.

Locomotives from Vulcan

In 1835, the company sent a purchase order to Vulcan Foundry of England (also known as Charles Tayleur & Company) for three 4-2-0 low boiler locomotives. The driving wheels were specified as fifty-four inches in diameter and the steam cylinders were to be ten inches by sixteen inches for greater power. The machines were:

16.	Kentucky	(4-2-0)	Vulcan #22
17.	Cincinnati	(4-2-0)	Vulcan #20
18.	Allen	(4-2-0)	Vulcan #21

Locomotives from Stevenson

Following the Vulcan purchase and shipment, the company received three locomotives from Robert Stevenson at Newcastle upon Tyne in England. These locomotives used the Edward Bury–designed inside iron-bar frame that was specifically called out in the Charleston & Hamburg specifications for the new locomotives. They were:

19.	Sumter	(4-2-0)	Stevenson
20.	Marion	(4-2-0)	Stevenson
21.	Ohio	(4-2-0)	Stevenson

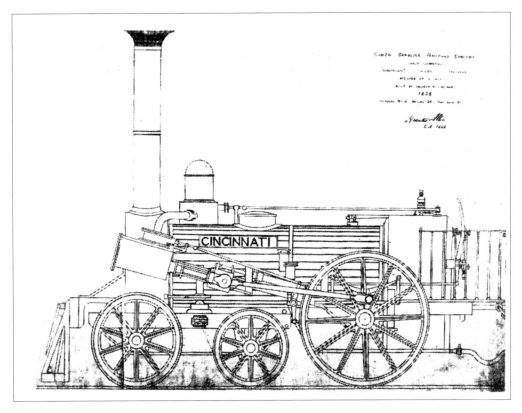

The C. Tayleur & Company of Warrington, England, built three locomotives in 1835 for the Charleston & Hamburg Rail Road. Named Cincinnati, Allen and Kentucky, these 4-2-0 machines featured a pilot and a fenced area for the engineer. The throttle was a large upright lever in back of the firebox. *Southern Railway Collection, Norfolk Southern.*

There were two additional locomotives purchased in 1835, one from the Rothwell Company and the other manufactured by the local Eason & Dotterer Company in Charleston. The wheel arrangement on these last two was unreported. They were:

22. H. Schultz   Rothwell
23. Washington   Eason & Dotterer

All of these locomotives were placed in service in 1835 with no apparent difficulties and the company was pleased with the performance of the British machines.

Cincinnati & Charleston Railroad (1835–1836)

Later the same year a new company, the Cincinnati & Charleston (C&C) Railroad, promoted by Robert Y. Hayne, revived the idea of a line from the C&H to Columbia and on to the Midwest. The C&C was chartered in December of 1835 to build a railroad

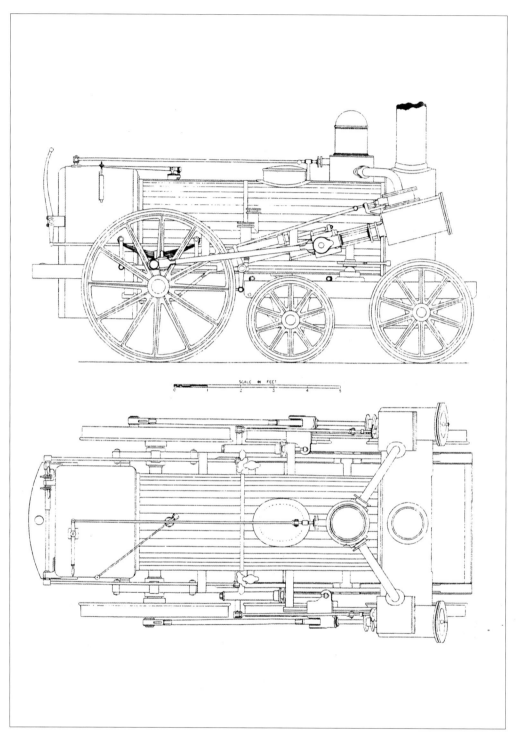

This detailed engineering drawing of the Cincinnati shows the off-set pistons that allowed the rods to be connected to the exterior of the fifty-four-inch-diameter driving wheels. This may be the first of this design on the C&HRR. *Author's collection*.

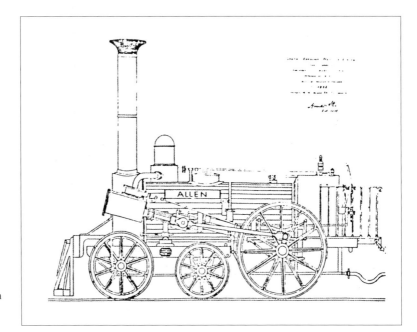

The Allen was a twin to the Cincinnati, and this appears to be the same drawing with the name Allen substituted. *Author's collection*.

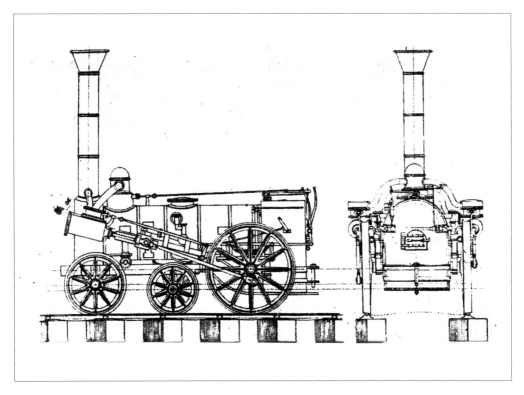

Robert Stephenson & Company built three locomotives named Sumter, Marion and Ohio for the Charleston & Hamburg in 1835. While very similar to the Tayleur locomotives, they lack a pilot and a platform for the engineer to stand. The stack is three sections high instead of two and the steam comes directly from the steam dome, instead of the steam dome base. *Author's collection*.

line from the Charleston & Hamburg Rail Road tracks near Midway to Columbia, then Knoxville in Tennessee and on to Covington, Kentucky, across the Ohio River from Cincinnati. The states of North Carolina and Tennessee also chartered this line, but Kentucky preferred the terminus to be at Louisville, as that gave the state a competitive advantage by not having the track going to Covington, across from Cincinnati in Ohio.

Building on the Columbia Railroad survey of 1835, the C&C decided to bend the line eastward north of Orangeburg to serve as part of a new, proposed branch to Camden, a town on the Fall Line. This required a new survey of the region around St. Matthews in early 1836.

Hayne, now president of the Cincinnati & Charleston, advocated the French Broad River route, in which the line was to cross the Blue Ridge Mountains, which blocked the route between Greenville and Asheville, by either of two routes to be surveyed. The first would cross a pass just east of Butt Mountain east of the Greenville Turnpike, in which the line would rise 1,102 feet in 18½ miles, and the second would use a pass at the headwaters of Reedy Patch Creek, rising 1,344 feet in 11 miles. This latter route would require the use of three to four inclined planes to lift the trains, similarly to the planes in use near Hamburg. Once over the Blue Ridge, the line could proceed to Asheville and then follow the French Broad River down along a reasonable grade to Newport, Tennessee, and an easy route down the valley to Knoxville. (The French Broad River route was built much later by the Western North Carolina and is in use by the Norfolk Southern today.)

John C. Calhoun, who resided at Clemson in Pickens County, proposed a radical new route in 1836 that would follow the Keowee River (which flowed into the Seneca River just upstream from Clemson) up and over the formidable Blue Ridge Mountains to the Tuckaseegee River, a branch of the Little Tennessee River in North Carolina, and then follow this to the Tennessee River itself. Calhoun had personally followed this route, which utilized portions of the old Cherokee Indian Trading Path. As he wrote the description to Hayne, the route would follow the ridge of land between the Savannah and Santee Rivers and cross the Blue Ridge summit from Whitewater creek to the "Tuckasiege."

Calhoun and Hayne became quite bitter in their rival support of the two different routes and the letters that were sent between the two men were later bound by John Cleveland under the title *Controversy between John C. Calhoun and Robt. Y. Hayne as to the Proper Route of a Railroad from South Carolina to the West* in 1913.

1836 – The C&H Rebuilds with T-Rail

The Cincinnati & Charleston charter was amended in December 1836 to reflect the desire of the state of Kentucky to have the new railroad terminate at Louisville. The new company, operating under this revised charter, was named Louisville, Cincinnati and Charleston Railroad. No construction had been done by the Cincinnati & Charleston other than survey work and endless discussions, which were swept aside. But the fate of the prosperous Charleston & Hamburg was to change dramatically the following year as a result of this new charter.

The Locomotives of 1836

The Charleston and Hamburg continued to have motive power shortages as some of the locomotives cycled into repair sheds and then emerged months later. However, the immediate need was much less and the company only purchased five locomotives in 1836. They were from Rothwell, the local Eason & Dotterer and from the new Baldwin Locomotive Works, which had a much improved reputation. They were:

24.	Tennessee		Rothwell
25.	Lafayette		Eason & Dotterer
26.	Franklin		Eason & Dotterer
27.	Philadelphia	(4-2-0)	Baldwin #23
28.	E.J. Ravenel	(4-2-0)	Baldwin #24

T-Section Rail Installed

By 1836, several ironworks in the North as well as in Europe were producing T-section rails for railroads. This was a singular improvement over the original strap rails laid on wood, or the replacement L-flange rails that the company had installed in 1834. The company ordered enough rails to relay the entire line and as rail was received at the Charleston wharves, the company began a rapid rebuilding program. The T-rail was able to be installed in such a way that the line did not have to be shut down except for limited periods of time in the work area where the rail replacement work was occurring. No modification

AUGUSTA DIRECTORY.

S. C. C. & R. R. COMPANY.

FARE REDUCED BETWEEN

CHARLESTON AND HAMBURG,

Eight Dollars through.

The Rail Road Passenger Train between Charleston and Hamburg. will leave as follows :

UPWARD.

Not to leave Charleston before	-	-		7 00	A. M.
"	"	Summerville,	-	-	-	8 30
"	"	Georges'	-	-	-	10 00
"	"	Branchville,	-	-		11 00
"	"	Blackville,	-	-	-	12 34	P. M.
"	"	Aiken,	-	-	-	2 45
Arrive at Hamburg not before	-	-	4 00

DOWNWARDS.

Not leave Hamburg, before		-	-	6 00	A. M.
"	"	Aiken,	-	-	-	7 30
"	"	Blackville,	-	-	-	9 15
"	"	Branchville,	-	-	-	11 00
"	"	Georges'	-	-		11 45
"	"	Summerville,	-	-	-	10 00
Arrive at Charleston not before	-	2 15	P. M.

Speed not over 25 miles an hour. To remain 20 minutes each, for breakfast and dinner, and not longer than 5 minutes for wood and water at any station.

To stop for passengers, when a WHITE FLAG is hoisted at either of the above stations ; and also at Sineaths, Woodstock, Inabinet's, 4 mile T. O., Rives', Grahams, Willerton, Winsor, Johnsons' and Marsh's T. O.

Passengers up will breakfast at Woodstock and dine at Aiken; down, breakfast at Aiken and dine at Charleston.

Circa 1836, this page from the Augusta directory shows the timetable for the Charleston & Hamburg along with descriptions of the stations that could flag a train to stop. The company is listed as the South Carolina Canal & Rail Road Company, the parent company of the railroad. *Author's collection.*

of the locomotives was required and the work went swiftly, although the cost was $440,620, which was less than the cost to install the earthen embankments two years earlier.

The Louisville, Cincinnati & Charleston Rail Road (1836–1843)

Robert Y. Hayne became the president of the new Louisville, Cincinnati & Charleston Rail Road (LC&CRR) in 1836. He had been governor of the state of South Carolina, Speaker of the House, attorney general and the first mayor of the city of Charleston.

Hayne wrote that the

> Western Railroad, building through Knoxville, Tennessee, would enter South Carolina through Spartanburg District with its point of destination Columbia, thence to connect with the Charleston & Hamburg Rail Road and that in response to applications from the inhabitants of Barnwell, Edgefield, Orangeburg, Columbia and Greenville, a reply had been made to Columbia that if the people of that town would build to connect with the Charleston & Hamburg Rail Road, the latter would, in all probability, take the branch off their hands at a premium.

The promoters of the LC&CRR were not able to raise sufficient funds from the general population to begin construction. To circumvent this problem, the LC&C established a separate corporation known as the Southwestern Railroad Bank. The bank charter made it clear that the bank was not liable for any debts of the LC&C, but the LC&C was liable for any bank debts.

The marriage of railroad and financial institution in the Southeastern United States was not unusual. The Georgia Rail Road & Banking Company, with its Georgia Railroad from Augusta to Decatur, and the Central Railroad and Banking Company, with its Central Railroad of Georgia from Savannah to Macon, both chartered in Georgia, were two examples that were long-lived. The GRR&B of Augusta is one of the major banking houses of the Southeast today.

The LC&CRR proposed to cross the Blue Ridge Mountains north of Gaffney by following the Broad River from Columbia and the French Broad River from Asheville to Knoxville. The line was to continue to Newport, Kentucky, opposite Cincinnati, a shift from Covington, which had been the earlier goal.

The pass through the Blue Ridge was to be either north of Greenville using a graded mainline or at Reedy Patch Creek on the Broad River, a location requiring three to four inclined planes to crest the mountains. Estimated cost for construction of the entire line was $11,804,046.

1837—The End of the Charleston & Hamburg Rail Road

The year 1837 saw several changes to the operations of the Charleston & Hamburg Rail Road. Seven new locomotives were acquired from American suppliers, with Baldwin Locomotive Works getting two of the orders. Meanwhile, it became clear that many of the original locomotives were worn out beyond the point where simple maintenance would make them viable. All four of the remaining South Carolina class were removed and scrapped. The company also removed all four-wheel freight cars from service and replaced them with cars riding on two four-wheel trucks, a design that permitted the cars to carry twice the load. Freight cars with two trucks are still in use today on American railroads. At the same time, the passenger cars, also built with four wheels, were replaced with new cars with two four-wheel trucks.

THE LOCOMOTIVES OF 1837

The railroad purchased seven new locomotives in 1837. However, this year was the first in which worn-out locomotives were removed from service. Six machines were taken from service. including all four of the South Carolina class. In some cases, the original locomotive name was transferred to one of the new machines.

Removed from service

2.	West Point	scrapped
3a.	Constitution (the rebuilt South Carolina)	scrapped
4.	Charleston	scrapped
5.	Barnwell	scrapped
6.	Edisto	scrapped
8.	Hamburg	scrapped

These two passenger cars on the Camden & Amboy Railroad in New Jersey were built about 1837, but were photographed in 1867. This design was typical of that which was adopted by the Charleston & Hamburg about 1838. *Author's collection.*

Acquired

The T.W. Smith Company was a new supplier of locomotives to the C&H and received an order for two machines. Similarly, McLeash & Smith was also new as a supplier and got an order for two machines.

29.	Wm. Penn		T.W. Smith
30.	Alexandria		T.W. Smith
31.	Edisto 2	(4-2-0)	Baldwin #92 (second use of this name)
32.	Barnwell 2	(4-2-0)	Baldwin #94 (second use of this name)
33.	Moultrie		Eason & Dotterer
34.	Vulcan		McLeash & Smith
35.	Charleston 2		McLeash & Smith (second use of this name)

The George S. Hacker Barrel Car

Colonel James Gadsden, one of the directors of the C&H, suggested that a new freight car could be built in the form of a hogshead barrel used to ship tobacco and this design would provide a number of advantages over the platform cars in use. George S. Hacker, the C&H master carpenter who was very familiar with the hogshead barrels, built the original prototype car for freight and had it rolled out in September of 1837. He later patented this totally new type of car in 1841.

The car was built at first to a twenty-one-foot length, but the design was later modified to the standard thirty-foot length. A single thirty-foot car could carry some forty-five bales of cotton.

The End of the Charleston & Hamburg Rail Road

On December 28, 1837, seven years and three days after the first trains operated on Christmas Day from Charleston to San Souci, the Louisville Cincinnati & Charleston Rail Road purchased the Charleston & Hamburg from its parent, the South Carolina Canal & Rail Road Company, for $2,400,000. This dramatic move gave the LC&C a viable railroad of more than one hundred miles, likely the most prosperous line in the country, to use as security in future financial manipulations. In the same stroke, the pioneering Charleston & Hamburg name passed from the public awareness and a hundred years later, the line was often thought to have been operated by the parent SCC&RR in historical references.

1838-1843 – The Louisville, Cincinnati & Charleston Rail Road Years

Hayne referred to the purchase of the Charleston & Hamburg in a report that he prepared two years later on September 16, 1839: "The necessity imposed upon us by our situation of becoming the purchasers of the Charleston & Hamburg Rail Road on credit." Hayne was still uncertain if the debt incurred had been worth the operating property. Robert Hayne died not many months later.

Once in control, the LC&C reevaluated the running time in use and dramatically reduced the time required to run from Hamburg to Charleston. The trains of the C&H were scheduled to take thirteen hours to make the run, but after the new management took control, the time was reduced to ten hours, leaving Charleston at 7:00 a.m. and arriving at Hamburg at 5:00 p.m. This allowed the company to put even more trains on the single-track line and to haul even more freight in a twenty-four-hour period.

The State of South Carolina agreed in 1838 to guarantee the issue of £200,000 of 5 percent sterling railroad bonds for every $500,000 worth of shares sold by the LC&C. These appear to be the first state-guaranteed railroad bonds ever issued. The bonds were sold in Europe by the Bank of the United States and were due in 1866. Soon after the issue, the Bank of the United States began to weaken, and a second group of bonds was issued by the House of Messrs Palmer, Mackillop, Dent & Co. of London. Each bond was signed by Robert Young Hayne, the president of the LC&C, and by his son, William E. Hayne, the state controller.

The bonds came due in 1866, but the War Between the States made it impossible for the State or the railroad to redeem them. A five-year delay was obtained and certificates of indebtedness were issued for past or future interest on the bonds.

THE NEW LINE TO COLUMBIA

The new company, well aware of the demand for service to Columbia, began construction of a new line starting at Branchville in 1838. This was a very different type of country to traverse, as the land was above the Pine Barrens and composed of sand hills and wide rivers as the land climbed to the Fall Line. The initial surveys indicated that the company would have to use inclines to get the trains up and down the slopes of the rivers between Orangeburg and the capital. This line was given the nickname Branchville & Columbia Railroad while under construction, but there was no company chartered or operated

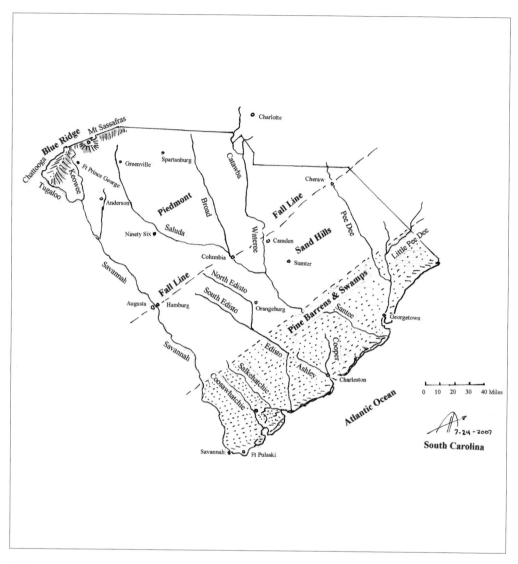

This map shows the distinctive regions that make up belts across the state of South Carolina. The pine barrens and swamps run from the coast back some forty miles to the sand hills. The Fall Line marks the shift from the Piedmont to the sand hills and the limit to navigation on the rivers within the state. The Piedmont is a rolling agricultural zone bounded by the Blue Ridge Mountains in the far northwest corner of the state, where Mount Sassafras rises up as the highest peak. *Map by author.*

under this name. This name is not to be confused with the Columbia & Branchville Railroad name used in 1834 by the Columbia Rail Road.

The "cotton crisis" of 1839 was named for the market collapse in which the price of cotton plummeted and directly affected the freight traffic on the line. With the market continuing to fall, the stockholders petitioned in September of 1840 for refunds of their investment. However, the company opened seventeen miles of new track in 1840 and ignored the requests.

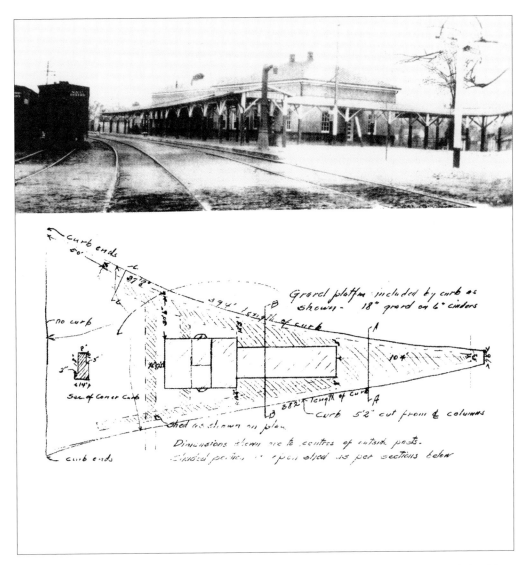

This photograph shows the back end of the depot at Branchville, as seen approaching from Columbia and bound for Charleston. The covered sheds allowed passengers to move from the Columbia Branch to the Aiken mainline to change trains. *Ties, Southern Railway Historical Society.*

JAMES GADSDEN

James Gadsden had been born in Charleston in 1788, the grandson of Christopher Gadsden, who had been captured by the British at Charleston and imprisoned at St. Augustine, Florida, for ten months. James went to Yale and later served in the U.S. Army as a lieutenant of engineers, then as aide under General Andrew Jackson in Florida. After the war, he was appointed federal commissioner by President James Monroe to resettle the Seminole Indians on reservations. Later, Gadsden had taken up the cause of nullification in 1832 and lost the support of now President Jackson. He returned to

Charleston to take up rice planting and was chosen to be the president of the Louisville, Cincinnati & Charleston Rail Road in 1839, serving until 1850.

Gadsden, while supporting the LC&C project to reach the Ohio River, proposed at several regional conferences that the South should establish a direct sea link to Europe, unite all the Southern railroads into one large system and build a new railroad from New Orleans to the Pacific Coast that would make the West economically dependent on the South. The preliminary study of the route showed that the most practical and direct route would be through Mexico, just below the new territories of New Mexico and Arizona, which had been purchased in February 1848 when Mexico, defeated in the Mexican War, gave up any claim to the Republic of Texas, Colorado, Utah, Nevada and California for $15 million. Overall, the land amounted to 200,000 square miles and was two-fifths of what had been the Republic of Mexico.

The Counterbalanced Aiken Planes Improvement

The elimination of the stationary steam engines on the inclined plane near Aiken in 1841 with a new locomotive-cable system was one of several improvements made by the LC&CRR. Here a locomotive would act as a counterweight for a counterbalanced cable funicular, which could haul one or more cars up or down on a parallel track. This new method of getting cars up or down the incline saved the company some $3,000.

Testing New Journals and Bearings for Axles

As the cars grew bigger and the freight weights grew heavier, the journal box that the axle end revolved in became more and more critical in its design to avoid mechanical breakdowns. One design by an innovative man named Elgers up north involved the use of iron boxes and steeled ends on the axles. Finding that the design worked well on LC&C eight-wheel freight cars, the company soon had the Elger journals installed on all of the cars of this type. The end of the axle was modified with a steel sleeve that was two inches in diameter and four and a half inches long. This was then forge welded in place. The bearing was made from a chill-hardened cast-iron material and the journal box used an oil box for the lubricant and a dust cover to keep dirt out.

The Elger journal was manufactured by the New Castle Manufacturing Company, but after some months, the company began to make them locally in Charleston. Instead of oil, the company resorted to using cheap tallow as the lubricant. Experience soon revealed that while the Elger journal was very practical when trains ran at a slow speed and the freight loads were light, they were not at all good as the trains began to run faster with heavier loads. A substitute was sought from the myriad designs on the market.

LOCOMOTIVES OF 1838

Only four new locomotives were ordered in 1838. In addition, the company removed the 1834 Stevenson 0-4-0 locomotive Edgefield from service.

Removed from Service

15.	Edgefield	Stevenson (scrapped)

Acquired New

36.	Branchville	Eason & Dotterer
37.	Reading	Eason & Dotterer
38.	Line Street	Unknown
39.	Experiment	Rogers, Ketcham & Grossvenor

COMPETITION: CENTRAL RAILROAD & BANKING COMPANY OF GEORGIA

We have seen that the Central of Georgia opened its first section of mainline, twenty-six miles headed northwest out of Savannah toward Macon, in May of 1838. While interesting, the railroad posed no threat to the LC&CRR.

LOCOMOTIVES OF 1839

With a portion of the new Branchline in service, the company acquired an additional four 4-2-0 locomotives, all from Baldwin, and ordered in 1839. They were:

40.	Robert Y. Hayne	(4-2-0)	Baldwin #132
41.	John Ravenel		Baldwin
42.	Buena Vista	(4-2-0)	Baldwin #73
43.	T.F. Tupper	(4-2-0)	Baldwin #126

COTTON BECOMES THE PRINCIPAL FREIGHT

The 1840 Annual Report revealed that the Louisville, Cincinnati & Charleston had hauled 60,000 bales of cotton in 1840, less than ten years after the first train operated on Christmas Day in 1830. This was equivalent to 9,600 tons over the Hamburg to Charleston line.

SOUTH CAROLINA. 25

SOUTH CAROLINA RAIL-ROAD,

BETWEEN CHARLESTON & HAMBURG, S. C. OPPOSITE AUGUSTA.

DEPARTS DAILY.—The following is the Winter Arrangement.

PASSAGE TO HAMBURG. UPWARD.			PASSAGE TO CHARLESTON. DOWNWARD.		
LEAVES			LEAVES		
Charleston at	7 o'clock	A. M.	Hamburg at	7 o'clock,	A. M.
Summerville ½ past	8 "	"	Aiken, ½ past	8 "	"
Georges ¼ "	10 "	"	Blackville ¼ "	10 "	"
Branchville	11 "	"	76 mile turn out,	12 "	M
Midway ¾ "	11 "	"	Midway ½ "	12 "	P. M.
76 mile turn out	12 "	M	Branchville ¼ "	12 "	"
Blackville ½ "	1 "	P. M.	Georges, "	1 "	"
Aiken ¾ "	3 "	"	Summerville, — ½ "	3 "	"
Arrives at Hamburg,	5 "	"	Ar. at Charleston, ¼ "	4 "	"
Distance,	136 miles.		Fare through, $0 75 cts.		

☞ The Summer arrangement differs from the Winter by one hour, as the Cars leave at 6 o'clock, and arrive at their destination at ½ past 6 o'clock, each way.

Speed not over 20 miles an hour. To remain 20 minutes each for breakfast and dinner. Five minutes to receive and deliver mails, and to take in wood and water.

Passengers will breakfast at Woodstock, and dine at Blackville.

To stop for passengers at all regular passenger stations when a white flag is hoisted as a signal.

Midway is 72 miles from Charleston—Fare $3 50, and 64 from Hamburg—Fare $3 75. Inabinets is 32½ miles from Charleston—Fare $1 62½, and 133 3-8 from Hamburg— Fare $5 12½. And from one intermediate Station to another, 5 cents per mile. Children under 12 years, and colored persons, half price.

At Branchville, passengers for Orangeburgh and Columbia leave the road.

☞ All baggage at the risk of the owner. Seventy-five pounds allowed. Company's Office, East Bay, Dewees Wharf.

RATES OF FREIGHT.

	per foot.	per 100 lb.		per foot.	per 100 lb.
To Branchville,	7 cts.	25 cts.	To Aiken,	13 cts. 45	cts.
To Blackville,	10 cts.	35 cts.	To Hamburg,	14 cts.	50 cts.

CHARGES.—For Labor and Storage, (not exceeding one week,) 3½ cts. per 100 lbs. or 1 ct. per cubic foot. After which, Storage to be charged at Charleston rates.

REGULATIONS.—1st. Freight will be forwarded agreeably to the order of time it is received, and must be in good order, and marked the name of the Station on the line it is to be left at, or it will not be received.

2d. All Freight must be paid for at the respective Depositories on its delivery.

Officers—President, T. Tupper. Directors, A. Blanding, A. Black, Ker Boyce, Dr. I. M. Campbell, Jos. Johnson, Chas. Edmondston, J. Hamilton, R. Y. Hayne, M. King, H. W. Peronneau. Secretary and Treasurer, Henry Ravenel. Assistant Secretary, W. H. Inglesby. Agent of Transportation, W. Robertson, jr. Master of Workshops, John Ross. Chief Agent, John King, jr. Receiver of Passengers and up Freight, John Heron. Receiver of down Freight, James Smith. Agent at Hamburg, A. B. Sturges.

Louisville, Charleston, and Cincinnatti Rail Road.

ROBERT Y. HAYNE, *Pres.* EDWARD W. EDWARDS, *Sec. and Treas.*
DIRECTORS.

For South Carolina.—Robt. Y. Hayne, A. Blanding, Mitchell King, Jas. Hamilton, Wade Hampton, Thomas F. Jones, B. T. Elmore, R. G. Mills, John Dunovant, Wm. Rier, John C. Calhoun, Ker Boyce
For North Carolina.—J. E. C. Hardy, Ch. Barring, T. J Forney, J. Rutherford.
For Tennessee.—Wm. B. Reese, J. G. M. Ramsey, T. W. Humes, A. E. Smith.
For Kentucky—Robert Wickliffe, Jas. Taylor, J. B Casey, W. H. Richardson.

Santee Canal Company.

Pres.—Jos. W. Turner. Sec. and Treas., John Duffus. Direct. Dr. Wm. Read. Jas. Lamb, George Buist, Wm. Burrow, Charles M'Beth, Harris Simons, S. N. Stevens, Robert T. Chisholm, John H. Tucker, Sam. W. Gibbes, Jacob R. Valk, Dr. I. M. Campbell.

This page from *McCarter's Almanac* of 1840 lists the "South Carolina Rail-Road," which was often used to refer to the Charleston & Hamburg Rail Road. A timetable, interesting footnotes and a freight rate table are included. The Louisville, Charleston & Cincinnati Rail Road seems to be a printer's error in switching the names. This company was busy making talk and trying to raise funds in 1840. The Santee Canal Company was still very viable, as there had been no attempt to build a railroad to Columbia yet. *Author's collection.*

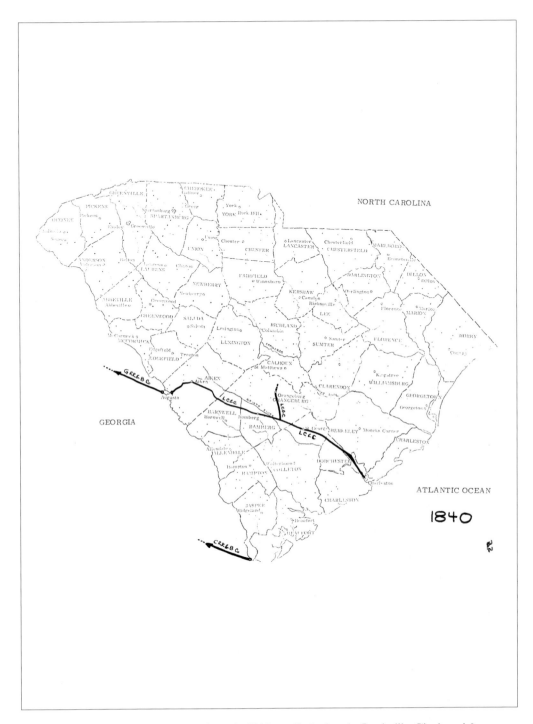

The railroad network in the lower southeast in 1840 was limited to the Louisville, Cincinnati & Charleston and two unconnected Georgia lines: the Georgia Rail Road & Banking Co. at Augusta and the Central Rail Road & Banking Co. at Savannah. *Map by author.*

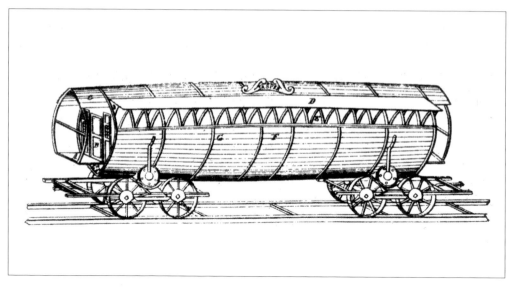

This is an original drawing from the 1841 Patent, #1,937, Railway Car by G.S. Hacker. Better known as a barrel car, the design was adaptable to freight or passenger use. *U.S. Patent Office, author's collection.*

The company had eliminated most of the small two-axle cars by this time and only six of these open freight cars were still on the roster. The basic fleet consisted of the iron boxcars designed in 1834 and the 1837 designed Hacker "barrel car."

HACKER BARREL PASSENGER CAR

The success of the Hacker hogshead barrel freight car led Gadsden to contemplate a passenger car with the same basic design. He again approached Hacker with his idea and Hacker got right to work on the modified design. Called the "barrel car," this passenger car was the first to be built anywhere in the country that had no resemblance to conventional coaches or wagons. The first car, some thirty feet long, was able to carry many more passengers than the small eight-wheel coaches. Following the first successful runs, Gadsden had the company produce a number of additional barrel cars for the long-distance trains.

There was a 2½-foot-long portico, or platform, at each end of the car. The passenger cabin had twenty glass windows, each 25 by 30 inches in size, which could be raised up above the opening. The walls were made of long staves, 5-inch wide boards, 30 feet long and 1¼ inches thick. These were grooved to fit together and the use of six iron hoops, 2 inches wide, held the boards in the barrel shape. The center of the car had a 9-foot diameter, while the ends tapered down to an 8-foot diameter.

Overall, both the freight and passenger types of barrel car were found to be much lighter on the road, and were cheaper to construct than the wagon type that had been in service from the beginning. The price was determined to be half that of a conventional car and the railroad reported that barrel cars "thrown from the Road are not so liable to be broken." In fact, when derailed, the cars would roll down the embankment without damage.

Hacker took out a patent that was granted as #1,937 on January 21, 1841, which was assigned to both the LC&C and the C&H railroads.

LOCOMOTIVES OF 1841

Only one locomotive was acquired in 1841. It was built by the Charleston & Hamburg itself.

44.   Orangeburg   C&HRR

COLUMBIA BECOMES THE SECOND TERMINAL

Construction of the LC&C was pushed forward by both the management and the State of South Carolina despite a market depression. The line was completed to Columbia in 1842 and managed to cross the rivers and the Fall Line without the use of inclines, which had proven to be a bottleneck on the original C&H line. The first passenger train reached Columbia on June 20, 1842, with the Robert Y. Hayne locomotive pulling the cars. The train was greeted by wildly cheering people who saw the arrival as a harbinger of a new and improved commerce. The first freight trains entered the city on July 1, only ten days later. The total cost of construction was $2,274,906.21 for the sixty-seven-mile-long branch. This high cost, together with the market depression, cancelled all of the plans to extend the line to the Ohio River.

The LC&C was now a two-pronged railroad that ran from Charleston to Branchville, with the old main continuing to Hamburg and the new branch headed north through Orangeburg to run to the state capital. Were it not for the market collapse, the line would have been able to finance line extensions in the next year, but faced with a new reality of little available capital, the company officers decided to recharter the line for a better definition of the goals.

LOCOMOTIVES OF 1842

One locomotive was scrapped in 1842 and two were rebuilt, with one renamed the same year.

Scrapped
14.   E. Horry   (0-4-0)   Stevenson (built 1834)

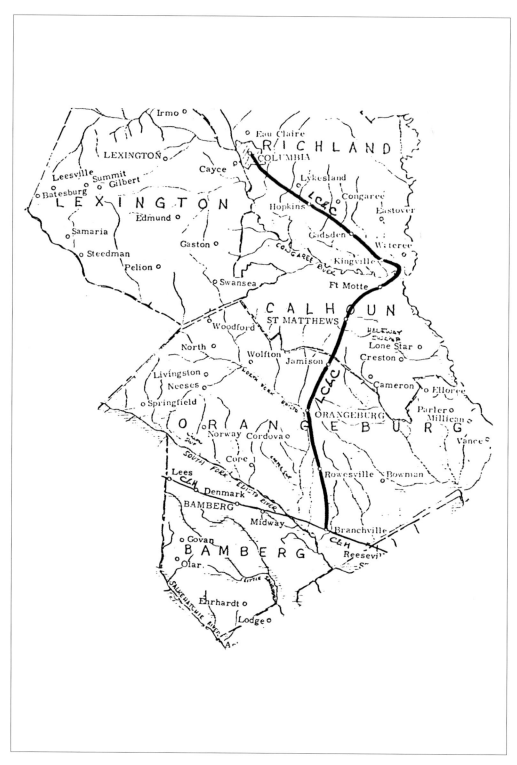

This map shows the route of the Louisville, Cincinnati & Charleston Columbia Branch from Branchville to Orangeburg, then St. Matthews, Fort Motte and Gadsden to Columbia. *Map by author.*

Rebuilt

12.	Columbia	(2-2-0)	Fenton (originally built 1834)
13a.	Camden	(0-4-0)	C&HRR (former #13, William Aiken)

1843 ANNUAL REPORT: COMMENTS ON THE BARREL CARS

The 1843 Annual Report mentioned that the barrel cars were "frequently condemned by strangers at first sight," but that these strangers soon appreciated the benefits of the odd design. The railroad thought it remarkable that live cinders would roll off the sides of the barrel cars without causing any damage. In one derailment, the barrel car rolled off the right-of-way without damage.

Three locomotives were scrapped in 1843. Two locomotives were rebuilt and one was renamed the same year.

Scrapped

24.	Tennessee		(built 1836)
27.	Philadelphia	(4-2-0)	Baldwin (built 1836)
36.	Branchville, Eason & Dotterer		(built 1838)

Rebuilt

17a.	Alabama	(2-4-0)	Vulcan (former #17, Cincinnati)
38.	Line Street		

Acquired New

45.	Camel	(0-6-0)	Baldwin #189
46.	Georgia	(0-6-0)	Baldwin #190
47.	Alabama 2	(0-6-0)	Baldwin #191 (second with this name)

1843-1860 – The South Carolina Rail Road

Once the plans to extend the Louisville, Cincinnati & Charleston on to Kentucky had been dropped, the name was no longer appropriate and, in fact, was misleading. However, the railroad did serve the greater part of the state. In addition, the company needed an infusion of new capital to begin additional expansion within the state. The South Carolina Canal & Railroad Company had a hefty treasury from the sale of the C&H back in 1836 for $2,400,000 and any thought of canal expansion was a dead issue in light of the success of the railroad system in South Carolina and other states. In fact, canal business had begun to fall off as soon as the LC&C began hauling cotton and other freight to Charleston from Columbia. The railroad approached the canal holding company and proposed a merger.

THE SOUTH CAROLINA RAIL ROAD (1843–1881)

The South Carolina Rail Road was formed by the merger of the SCC&RR Company and the LC&CRR on December 19, 1843. Colonel James Gadsden continued on as president of the new company. The tracks of the new SCRR ran from Charleston to Hamburg, South Carolina, across the Savannah River from Augusta, Georgia, and from Branchville, South Carolina, on the mainline up to Orangeburg and on to Columbia, the state capital.

COMPETITION: THE CENTRAL OF GEORGIA

The Central Rail Road and Banking Company of Georgia completed its line through to Macon, Georgia, on October 13, 1843, just two months before the formation of the South Carolina Rail Road. Since the line headed west to Macon, it held little threat to the SCRR.

LOCOMOTIVES OF 1844

One locomotive, the H. Schultz, built by Rothwell, was scrapped in 1844 after nine years of service.

Scrapped

22.   H. Schultz   Rothwell (built 1835)

The South Carolina Rail Road purchased three new locomotives in 1844. Included was the fiftieth locomotive for the combined C&H, LC&C and SCRR lines.

Acquired New

48.	Louisiana	(0-6-0)	Baldwin #202
49.	Arkansas	(0-6-0)	Baldwin #203
50.	Tennessee	(0-6-0)	Baldwin #204

By 1845, the new line owned 22 locomotives, of which 16 were in constant use, as well as 18 passenger cars and 283 freight cars. One locomotive was assigned to the inclined planes near Aiken. This locomotive worked one side of the two planes counterbalancing the cars that were raised or lowered by a cable attached to the steam engine. This machine would descend the right-hand plane as two eight-wheel cars carrying 120 bales of cotton were raised on the left-hand plane. The locomotive would then steam back up the hill and the rope would be lowered for two more cars of cotton. The average train consisted of twenty cars and it took fifteen minutes to make a round trip on the planes. Therefore, it took two and a half or more hours to transfer a train from the foot of the plane to the top.

THE AMERICAN (4-4-0) LOCOMOTIVE DESIGN

Colonel Gadsden, the president of the SCRR, contacted Baldwin in Philadelphia, who was operating as Baldwin & Whitney in these years, in 1845 to build a set of three 4-4-0s, a design that would have great impact on the railroad industry. Baldwin had little interest in this proposed wheel arrangement, but changed his mind after viewing the first trials of Antelope, the first eight-wheel locomotive to be built. The machine had sixty-inch drivers and weighed fifteen tons. Baldwin quickly realized that the machine could outperform anything the factory had on the floor. He was "more than pleased with its appearance and action than any engine he had turned out." The design was one that became so popular with the railroad industry that it was given the name "American" type.

The two other 4-4-0 locomotives, Comet and Dolphin, were finished and the three sprinters were shipped to Charleston. The South Carolina Rail Road assigned them to haul fast passenger trains between Charleston and the two terminals in the sand hills above the Fall Line.

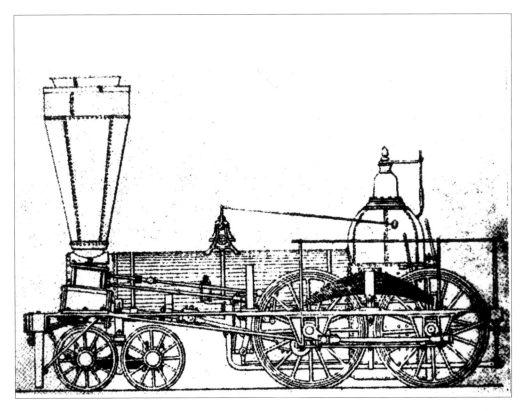

This was the first 4-4-0 eight-wheel locomotive built by Baldwin for any railroad. The South Carolina Rail Road took the first three of these 1845 locomotives, which were named Antelope, Comet and Dolphin. Note the flared stack and the blunt pilot on the front. *Author's collection.*

LOCOMOTIVES OF 1845

Acquired New

51.	Texas	(0-6-0)	Baldwin #233
52.	Antelope	(4-4-0)	Baldwin #240 (first eight-wheel locomotive)
53.	Comet	(4-4-0)	Baldwin #241
54.	Dolphin	(4-4-0)	Baldwin #242

Rebuilt

9a.	Edgefield 2	(4-2-0)	Baldwin (built in 1834 as E.L. Miller)
31a.	Edisto	(4-2-0)	Baldwin (built in 1837 as Edisto)

The Charleston & Hamburg

Competition: The Georgia Rail Road & Banking Company

Construction of the Georgia Rail Road west from Augusta to Athens and on to Terminus, an unsettled area near Decatur that became Atlanta, was very slow. Even with ten miles in operation in January of 1837, Terminus was not reached until September of 1845. No connection existed with the South Carolina Rail Road across the Savannah River in Hamburg until 1852. For the seven intervening years, goods that were interchanged had to be taken across the bridge by wagon.

Competition: The Wilmington & Manchester

A new railroad, the Wilmington & Manchester Railroad, was chartered in North Carolina after the port city observed the success of the South Carolina, the Central of Georgia and the Georgia Rail Road in carrying huge amounts of freight from remote areas to the sponsor cities. Wilmington, like Charleston, had a good harbor but no access to the inland areas. However, instead of building toward Raleigh, Wilmington set its sights on Manchester, one of the largest cities in South Carolina at that time, which was situated on the Wateree River at the Fall Line.

The company quickly completed a survey through Mullins, Florence and Sumter to Manchester (which in the mid-twentieth century had been reduced to a signpost for Sumter Junction). Construction began in 1848 and was completed in 1853.

Extension: The Greenville & Columbia Railway

With the South Carolina Rail Road tied up with improvements to the two mainlines and building a branch line to Camden, there was no way for the company to build additional trackage to Greenville in the upper Piedmont area. Yet the people of Greenville and the towns in between were anxious to have a railroad into their area. An independent company, the Greenville & Columbia Railway, was chartered in December 1846 to build just such an extension of the SCRR from Columbia into western South Carolina. Surveys were made in 1847 and 1848 that proposed various terminals for the line from Anderson to Greenville, but like many others starting up, there was no financial support from the public. Without public support, the project seemed doomed until the State of South Carolina offered a grant of $250,000 in South Carolina Rail Road bonds in exchange for thirteen thousand shares of Greenville & Columbia stock.

Extension: The Charlotte & South Carolina Railroad

The Charlotte & South Carolina Railroad was also chartered in December of 1846. The company had initially proposed to build from Charlotte south to Camden, but the people of Columbia pledged a sum of money that prompted the company to shift the

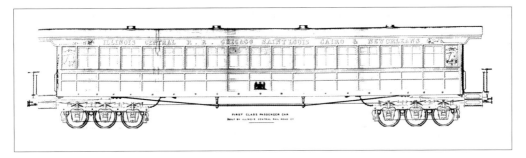

A typical twelve-wheel passenger car of 1858, this Illinois Central design represents what the South Carolina Rail Road cars would have looked like when introduced. *Author's collection.*

terminal from Camden to Columbia and to build north toward Charlotte. The C&SC chose a route following a ridge northward that limited the number of river crossings that had to be made. However, the company was not well off and it soon approached the state for financial support to begin construction. The State of South Carolina granted $250,000 in South Carolina Rail Road bonds in 1848 equal to the grant given to the Greenville & Columbia.

Twelve-wheel Passenger Cars

The 1846 Annual Report mentioned that the South Carolina Rail Road was experimenting with new, heavier passenger cars equipped with two three-axle trucks to distribute the load. These were referred to as the twelve-wheel passenger cars.

Locomotives of 1846

Acquired New

55.	Southerner		SCRR
56.	Falcon	(4-4-0)	Baldwin #267

Extension: Spartanburg & Union Railway

The Spartanburg & Union Railway was chartered in December of 1847 by the people of Spartanburg, who desired a link to the sea. Dismayed that nearby Greenville on the west and Charlotte on the east were to have direct rail lines to Columbia, Spartanburg was determined not to be left behind. The state was called on to lend financial support and gave the line grants in 1850 and 1852 before construction began in 1853.

The Juno, which was built for the Baltimore & Ohio in 1848 by Ross Winnans, had an earlier twin named Rough & Ready that was sent to the South Carolina Rail Road in 1847. The tender is somewhat bigger than the locomotive to permit longer runs between service points. *Author's collection.*

LOCOMOTIVES OF 1847

Acquired New

57.	Nashville		SCRR
58.	Atlanta	(0-8-0)	Baldwin #296
59.	Buena Vista 2	(0-8-0)	Baldwin #297 (exploded April 1848)
60.	Coosaw	(0-8-0)	Baldwin #298
61.	Wateree	(0-8-0)	Baldwin #300
62.	Rough & Ready	(4-4-0)	Ross-Winans (based on B&O Juno design)
63.	John C. Calhoun	(4-2-0)	Norris
64.	Cerro Gordo	(4-2-0)	Norris
65.	Rio Grande	(0-8-0)	Baldwin #295
66.	Chattanooga	(0-8-0)	Baldwin #301

COMMENTS ON THE JOURNEY FROM ORANGEBURG TO AUGUSTA IN 1849

Lossing, in his *Pictorial Field-Book of the Revolution*, mentions riding on the South Carolina Rail Road in January of 1849.

> *The rail-way journey from Orangeburg to Augusta was extremely monotonous in scenery and incident. At Branchville, on the banks of the Edisto, where the rail-way from Charleston connects, the immobility into which the passengers were subsiding was disturbed by the advent of a "turban'd Turk" in full Oriental costume. His swarthy complexion, keen eye, flowing black beard, broad turban, tunic and trowsers [sic] made him the "observed of all observers" and kept the passengers awake for an hour for "Yankee*

curiosity" was too busy to allow drowsiness. "When I came, and whither I go, ye know not" were as plain as a written phylactery upon his imperturbable features and I presume the crowd who gathered around him in the street at Augusta knew as little of his history and destiny as we. It is pleasant sometimes to see curiosity foiled.

The scenery by the way-side alternated between oozy swamps embellished with cypresses, cultivated fields, and extensive forests of oak and pine, garnished occasionally by a tall broad leaved magnolia. The country was perfectly level through Barnwell District, until we passed Aiken into Edgefield, and turned toward Silver Bluff on the Savannah River, when we encountered the sand hills of that region. These continued until we reached the termination of the road at Hamburg, on the northern bank of the Savannah opposite Augusta. There we were packed into huge omnibuses and conveyed to the city across Schultz's bridge. It was sunset—a glorious sunset like those at the north in September. A stroll about the city by moon-light that evening with a Northern friend residing there was really delightful for the air was balmy and dry and the moon and stars had nothing of the crisp piercing and glittering aspect which they assume in a clear January night in New England.

Early on the following morning we rode over to Hamburg and ascended to the summit of Liberty Hill, a lofty sand bluff three fourths of a mile from the river. Flowers were blooming in the gardens on its brow and over its broad acres green grass and innumerable cacti were spread.

Lossing evidently changed trains at Branchville, and was unable to cross the Savannah River by rail at that time.

THE CAMDEN BRANCH, 1848

The Wateree River basin, a heavily forested and swamp-filled area extending north from the confluence of the Wateree with the Congaree River near Kingville on the SCRR's Columbia Branch, offered a natural water-level right-of-way to Camden on the Fall Line. The steady market for naval stores and the potential shipment of market goods to Camden prompted the construction of the Camden Branch in 1845.

This new line was built from Kingville through Wateree, where it turned northward along the east side of the Wateree Swamp to run up to Camden. The swamp forced the SCRR to build more than four miles of trestlework, the construction of which was hampered by the frequent flooding of the area. This trestle was the longest work of its type in the United States when completed in February of 1848.

The Camden Branch itself was completed in October of 1848 after three long years of backbreaking labor. The labor was supplied by the local planters and plantation owners of the Sumter area, who were suffering from the effects of a depression that lasted from 1837 to 1845. By contracting with the railroad for their slave labor, the depleted fields were permitted to lie fallow for a few years and the planters were supported by the railroad construction payments.

The South Carolina Rail Road depot at Camden mimics the architecture of the depots in Charleston. *Southern Railway collection; Ties, Southern Railway Historical Society.*

The stations of the new branch were Junction (now called Kingville), Manchester, Middleton, Claremont, Sanders, Boykin and Camden. The first trains left Camden at 6:00 a.m. and arrived at Junction at 8:15. The return trip left Junction at 2:45 p.m. and arrived back at Camden at 5:15. Within the first three months of operation, the branch carried more than thirty thousand bales of cotton south to Charleston.

THE BUENA VISTA EXPLODES

Accidents continued to plague the line off and on through the years. The boiler of the new Buena Vista (second), a Baldwin 0-8-0 (serial number 297), exploded early on April 9, 1848, while in service. The engineer, twenty-two-year-old George Artope, and two firemen, Henry Cammer and Cecil Conrad, were killed in the accident. Artope was buried at the Cathedral Church of St. Luke and St. Paul at 126 Coming Street in Charleston, where his stone was discovered in 1972 covered with grime. When the stone was cleaned and the manner of his death uncovered, the first thought was that Artope had been killed by the explosion of the Best Friend, but the Southern Railway System explained that the Buena Vista locomotive had exploded in 1848, many years after the Best Friend incident.

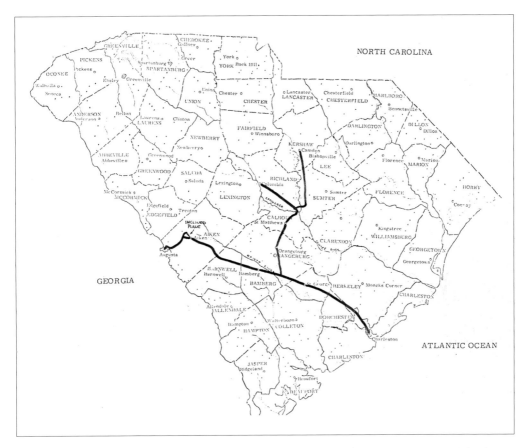

The completed South Carolina Rail Road ran west to Hamburg, north and west to Columbia and north to Camden. All three cities were on the Fall Line and were originally established as transfer points for agricultural goods in farm wagons from the Piedmont to the flatboats and steamboats of the navigable river system. *Map by author.*

LOCOMOTIVES OF 1848

Acquired New

67. Memphis   (4-4-0)   Baldwin #352

EXTENSION: THE CHERAW & DARLINGTON

Charleston financial support was used to build a new line north to Cheraw. The Cheraw & Darlington planned to build north from Florence—a new town on the Wilmington & Manchester—to Cheraw on the Fall Line at the Pee Dee River, where they could serve the busy lumber and naval stores processing area. The C&D was chartered in 1849 just after the W&M had started construction and began building their own line in 1854.

EXTENSION: THE GREENVILLE & COLUMBIA RAILWAY

The Greenville & Columbia Railway purchased thirty-four miles of used flange rail from the old C&H mainline at $45 a ton in return for SCRR bonds that the State of South Carolina had granted the G&C. The flange rail was being replaced in parts with the newer T-rail. Construction began in Columbia and continued north toward Greenwood. An additional grant of $75,000 in SCRR stock was made by the state in December 1849 when the state legislators could see the G&CR work trains from the capitol windows.

As the line advanced, it was planned to run a branch from Belton some ten miles over to Anderson, the county seat of Anderson County.

LOCOMOTIVES OF 1849

Acquired New

68.	Mississippi	(4-2-0)	Norris
69.	Charleston 3	(4-2-0)	Norris (replaced the 1837 Charleston)
70.	Cherokee	(4-2-0)	Norris
71.	California	(4-2-0)	Norris
72.	Flying Dutchman	(4-2-0)	Norris

1850—COTTON FREIGHT EXPANDS EXPONENTIALLY

Only ten years after carrying 60,000 bales of cotton in 1840 on the single mainline between Hamburg and Charleston, the South Carolina Rail Road, now with both the extension to Columbia and the branch up to Camden operating, in 1850 carried 285,000 bales of cotton during the year, nearly five times (4.75) the amount of 1840. This was equivalent to 45,600 tons of cotton and provided a huge incentive for the company to continue its expansion into new markets.

PASSENGER EQUIPMENT

Passenger cars were given names in place of numbers in the early years of the South Carolina Rail Road. In 1850 a list of the cars would have included Edwin P. Starr, General Worth, Colonel Dickinson, Washington, John C. Calhoun, Colonel P.M. Butler, Henry Clay, Major A. Black and Hampton. Some of these cars were equipped with six-wheel trucks and, in a few cases, with eight-wheel trucks.

THE WATEREE RIVER TRESTLE COLLAPSE OF 1850

The four-mile-long Wateree River Trestle on the Camden Branch collapsed over three miles of its structure in October of 1850 "due to a grossly erroneous plan of construction." A freight train of twelve cars loaded with bales of cotton from Camden to Charleston was passing over the trestlework when the spans went down. Some eight months were required to replace the collapsed section and strengthen the remaining mile.

It was soon evident that the high expense of rebuilding the Wateree River Trestle was not likely to be recovered from the revenue from the new line, as it was not as great as originally predicted. The company searched for some means to alleviate the financial predicament, but none was evident at first.

GADSDEN RETIRES

James Gadsden left the presidency of the South Carolina Rail Road in 1850 to return to Charleston. Three years later, President Franklin Pierce appointed Gadsden as minister to Mexico and he quickly negotiated a new Gadsden Treaty with Santa Ana, Mexican dictator, in 1853 that moved the U.S. border farther south for an agreed $10 million. This 45,535 acres was nearly as large as Pennsylvania, but the deal did not sit well with the Mexicans and dictator Santa Ana was thrown out and banished from Mexico. Gadsden was recalled for getting involved with Mexican internal politics. Seventy-year-old James Gadsden died in 1858 in Charleston on Christmas Day, twenty-eight years after the first train ran on the Charleston & Hamburg.

Years later, the Gadsden Treaty property allowed the Southern Pacific to build its railroad line from El Paso, the terminal of the Texas & New Orleans, to California without crossing any significant mountain range. Although not the first railroad to California, the route had significant economic benefits to Louisiana, but not to the South, which had suffered the loss of the Civil War in 1865.

Gadsden's direction of the LC&C and the SCRR over the thirteen years he held the presidency was marked with remarkable change for what had been the Charleston & Hamburg Rail Road. Some thirty-five new locomotives had been purchased and the rail system now stretched from Charleston to Hamburg, Columbia and Camden, and had controlling interest in the new lines building toward Anderson, Greenville and Spartanburg. Aside from Horatio Allen, Gadsden was the most influential man to direct the affairs of the line.

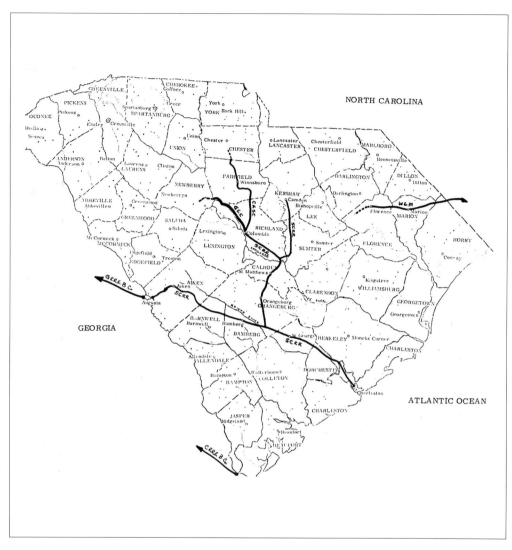

A map of the railroads in South Carolina in 1850 shows the South Carolina Rail Road with the original mainline to Augusta, a branch to Columbia and a second branch to Camden serving the central part of the state. The Georgia Rail Road and the Central of Georgia run west from Augusta and Savannah, respectively. Building westward from Wilmington, North Carolina, is the new Wilmington & Manchester in the eastern part of the state, and the new Greenville & Columbia and the Charlotte & South Carolina are building north from the state capital. *Map by author.*

Locomotives of 1850

Acquired New

73.	Robert Y. Hayne 2		Norris
74.	E.H. Elmore		Norris
75.	Wm. Lowndes	(0-6-0)	Baldwin #391

76.	Langdon Cheves		Rogers Ketcham & Grosvenor
77.	Wm. Cummings	(4-4-0)	Baldwin #399

FAST TRAINS

In 1851, the SCRR was operating an 8:00 a.m. train out of Charleston that was broken into separate sections at Branchville and again at Kingville to arrive at Hamburg and Columbia at 3:30 p.m. and at Camden at 4:30. But the prize of the fleet was the 11:30 a.m. express train to Hamburg, which took six hours, made with no stops along the way, and carried no freight.

The fastest run of all was made on June 18, 1851, when the 136 miles were run in four hours and forty-five minutes with six stops. R.Y. Hayne and A. Spencer were engineers on this unique run to Hamburg.

LOCOMOTIVES OF 1851

Acquired New

78.	George McDuffie	Norris
		(named after former governor of South Carolina, 1834–36)
79.	D.E. Huger	Norris
80.	V.K. Stevenson	Norris
81.	Ariel (SCRR 15)	Norris
82.	Sylphide	Norris
83.	James L. Pettigru	Newcastle (exploded 1851, scrapped)

THE LOSS OF THE JAMES L. PETTIGRU

In an accident similar to that of the Buena Vista, the James L. Pettigru (#86), a brand-new Newcastle locomotive, exploded only months after delivery, killing its crew of three. A second Newcastle locomotive arrived in 1852 (#87) and was given the same name.

THE BLUE RIDGE RAILROAD

The State of South Carolina directly supported the Blue Ridge Railroad, which was chartered in December of 1852 to build a line across the Blue Ridge Mountains to Knoxville, Tennessee. This still seemed viable in light that no rail connection existed at Augusta with the Georgia Rail Road and its partners that were operating a line through to the Ohio River. A New York construction company was hired to build the line, but was dismissed after two years for accomplishing nothing more than rudimentary grading of some right-of-way. A new company was hired the next month and within seven months rail had been laid from Anderson, newly connected to the state's railway system by the Greenville & Columbia road, running north to Pendleton.

A third work party was clawing away at the Stump House Mountain, high in the range north of Walhalla. Tunnel Hill, South Carolina, had a population of fifteen hundred workers, and in the six years from 1853 to 1859 the state poured over $1 million into the one-and-a-half-mile tunnel project. With two-thirds of the tunnel completed, the work stopped cold with a toll of $2.5 million. The state had purchased a railroad running from Anderson north to Walhalla and a $1 million hole in the ground.

Extension: The Charlotte & South Carolina Railroad

The Charlotte & South Carolina Railroad reached Charlotte in November of 1852, completing a branch that served as a friendly connection to the South Carolina Rail Road. Built north through Winnsboro, Chester and Rock Hill, the line linked several important county seats in the upper Piedmont area.

Extension: The Kings Mountain Railroad

The Kings Mountain Railroad was chartered in December of 1849 by the people of Yorkville (now York), South Carolina, who were bypassed by the route of the Charlotte & South Carolina. This was the second of several county seat railroads to be built and it was opened in September of 1852 from Chester to Yorkville after the C&SC reached Rock Hill.

Extension: The Greenville & Columbia Railway

The Greenville & Columbia tracks reached Greenwood early in 1852 and continued north and east to reach the terminal at Greenville in December of 1852. The completed line included a branch from Belton west to Anderson, the county seat of Anderson County. The next year, in answer to the requests of the people of Abbeville, the G&C built a branch line west from Cokesbury (now known as Hodges) to the county seat of Abbeville County.

The state of South Carolina controlled the G&C until 1870, although the South Carolina Rail Road used it as a natural extension to develop a considerable marketing interchange business. In other words, the South Carolina Rail Road operated the Greenville & Columbia as a line of its own, and in fact, it was.

LOCOMOTIVES OF 1852

Acquired New

84.	James L. Pettigru 2	Newcastle
85.	Fawn	Norris (returned 1854)
86.	Horatio Allen	New Jersey Locomotive
87.	Humming Bird	New Jersey Locomotive
88.	James Adger	Norris
89.	John Fraser	Norris
90.	Joseph Johnson (SCRR7)	Norris
91.	Velocity	Rogers, Ketcham & Grosvenor (sold to G&C, 1856)
92.	Gazelle	Rogers, Ketcham & Grosvenor
93.	Thomas Bennett	Norris
94.	Wm. Aiken 2 (SCRR8)	Norris
95.	Edward Corren	Newcastle

The numbering of the South Carolina Rail Road locomotives took place after the War Between the States. For clarity, the surviving locomotives are listed with that SCRR number, but only the name was used until after the war. Locomotives without SCRR numbers were sold, scrapped or destroyed in the war.

WILMINGTON & MANCHESTER RAILROAD CONNECTION: JOINT OWNERSHIP OF THE CAMDEN BRANCH

The construction of the Wilmington & Manchester Railroad from Wilmington, North Carolina, was completed to the South Carolina Rail Road's Camden Branch at Manchester (Sumter Junction) in 1853. Manchester was a major trading point that had been established at the Fall Line, where goods could be transferred to steamboats. Originally Manchester had been more of a western frontier town with minimal law enforcement and a large number of taverns and other establishments. The arrival of the South Carolina Rail Road in 1848 dramatically reduced steamboat shipments and the frontier-like character began to fade from Manchester.

The arrival of the W&M at Wateree Junction provided the SCRR with a direct rail connection to North Carolina via Florence, although the company was not expecting to receive or ship much freight over this competitive line. However, the failure of the Camden Branch to become self-supporting from the freight revenue, plus the debt incurred from rebuilding the Wateree River Trestle, had made the branch the least productive for the company. The W&M quickly expressed an interest in securing both a direct connection to the Columbia Branch and to obtaining trackage rights to Camden. After some negotiating, the two companies agreed to the formation of a fifty-fifty joint ownership of the Camden line east of Kingville. Since the line was already in place, this agreement provided much-needed cash to the South Carolina Rail Road without any expense involved. A wye was built on twelve-foot timber trestlework at Wateree Junction. This wye, a triangular track pattern, allowed trains from Kingville to turn north to Camden or continue straight on to Sumter. Similarly, trains from Camden could turn west to Kingville or east to Sumter. It is known that W&M trains normally ran straight on from Sumter to Kingville to make a connection with the SCRR trains from Charleston or Columbia. In fact, the SCRR ran at least one train each way to and from Columbia to Kingville to accommodate this traffic.

It is believed that this agreement may have led to W&M trains proceeding on to Columbia from Kingville for an undetermined period and that in a quid pro quo, certain SCRR trains were permitted to go from Kingville to Sumter over the W&M tracks.

1853—INTERCHANGE WITH THE GEORGIA RAIL ROAD AT AUGUSTA

The South Carolina Rail Road was finally able to purchase a license for $150,000 in July of 1852 from the City of Augusta, which gave the railroad permission to bridge the Savannah River into that city and to build a connection through the streets to reach the Georgia Rail Road. The money was jointly put up by the SCRR (50 percent) and the Georgia Rail Road, the Nashville & Chattanooga Railroad and the Memphis & Charleston Railroad (17 percent each), since all four companies saw the connection as extremely worthwhile. The bridge was completed in the summer of 1853, but there was still a gap of one mile down the city streets between the SCRR terminal and the Georgia RR terminal. Although the city allowed the track connection to be made, the freight cars were restricted to being transferred using only horsepower until 1857, when the city finally permitted locomotives to interchange freight between the lines. The opposition of local merchants and citizens to the operation of locomotives on the city streets forced this restriction through the city council for four years. Although it may seem restrictive, it was far more practical than the transloading of freight into teamsters' wagons and hauling the goods across town and over the bridge to Hamburg. Goods bound from one line to the other remained in the closed and locked freight cars and traveled through to the receiver.

The Georgia RR had been operating westward out of Augusta since 1837 and the gap at Augusta proved to be a great hindrance to both companies. With through service, the link provided a continuous railway from Charleston to the Ohio River via the South Carolina Rail Road to Augusta, the Georgia RR to Atlanta, the Western & Atlanta RR to Chattanooga, the Nashville & Chattanooga RR to Nashville and the Louisville & Nashville Railroad to the Ohio River at Louisville. Sleeping car service was initiated at this time between Atlanta and Charleston on through overnight trains.

The SCRR owned 62 locomotives, 59 passenger cars and 790 freight cars. Its investments included the jointly owned Camden Branch and an interest in the Charlotte & South Carolina Railroad, the Greenville & Columbia Railway, the

Wilmington & Manchester Railroad, the North Carolina Railroad and the Blue Ridge Railroad. This financial connection foretold the eventual formation of railroad systems that blossomed first in the South and then spread across the nation.

THE BYPASS OF THE AIKEN PLANES—1853

The inclined planes near Aiken became a much greater burden on the company as trains were disassembled, raised or lowered, and then reassembled to proceed on down the line. A new route was surveyed that would allow trains to bypass the planes and proceed directly past the bluffs at Aiken. The new mainline swung well to the east and then slowly down a descending grade to the bottom of the planes. This new route managed to use one-third less track and permitted direct service by both the freight and passenger trains. This construction and renovation was completed in February of 1853. As such, it marked a remarkable improvement and resulted in a far shorter scheduled time to travel from Charleston to Augusta.

SABOTAGE OF THE NIGHT EXPRESS

In 1853, the night express running from Charleston to Columbia ran off the track at Cattle Creek and the engine and the first four cars plunged thirty feet to the stream bed below. The accident was laid to "some evil disposed person or persons having maliciously placed two bars of old flange iron in such a position as to lead the train off the track."

LOCOMOTIVES OF 1853

1853 was the occasion of South Carolina receiving the one hundredth locomotive built for the combined C&H, LC&C and SCRR lines.

96.	Mayor of Augusta		Anderson & Southern
97.	South Carolina 2		Anderson & Southern
98.	Wade Hampton (SCRR16)		Norris
99.	J.G. Ramsey		Norris
100.	Brian Boraimbe		Norris
101.	Tiger		Anderson & Southern
102.	North Carolina		Norris
103.	Andrew Wallace	(2-6-0)	Baldwin #539
104.	E.J. Shannon	(0-6-0)	Baldwin #540

105.	A.E. Mills	(0-6-0)	Baldwin #541
106.	J.A. Whiteside	(0-6-0)	Baldwin #542
107.	Senator Butler		Norris
108.	Governor Manning (SCRR9)		Norris
109.	W.H. Thomas (SCRR10)		Norris
110.	J.O. Petsch		Norris (sold to S&U 1859)

EXTENSION: SPARTANBURG & UNION RAILWAY

Construction finally began on the Spartanburg & Union Railway after a long struggle to raise funds, including two grants from the State of South Carolina. Still, with a tight budget, the company had to request a third loan in 1858.

EXTENSION: THE CHARLESTON & SAVANNAH RAILROAD

The two rival seaports at Savannah and Charleston had little in common as far as shipping or receiving trade goods. Still, a rail connection between the two cities seemed to be a worthwhile endeavor in building a rail network across the state. The Charleston & Savannah was chartered in December of 1853. Construction began in 1856 after two complete surveys had been made through the Lowcountry. Work was not easily done in the swamps and estuarial waters and there were a number of major rivers to cross, namely the Edisto, Ashepoo, Salkehatchee, Combahee and Savannah.

THE SECOND COLLAPSE OF THE WATEREE TRESTLE—1854

The Wateree Trestle collapsed once again in 1854 as a train was crossing and several patrons were killed or severely injured. The structure was quickly replaced, but a year later the railroad was forced by the state to install a stationary bridge section in the trestlework over the main channel of the Wateree River to clear steamboats of thirty-five feet in height. In addition, the SCRR had to pay the steamboat companies for the installation of smokestack hinges that permitted the boats to pass beneath the new bridge.

LOCOMOTIVES OF 1854

Seven new locomotives were acquired in 1854, with four from Norris and three from Baldwin. Most mysterious was the loss of the Alexander Black, which disappeared in 1861, most likely due to reshuffling of equipment during the early days of the war.

111.	Fawn 2 (SCRR11)		Norris
112.	Gazelle 2		Norris
113.	Mayor Hutchinson (SCRR13)		Norris
114.	Mitchell King (SCRR14)		Norris
115.	Governor Morehead (SCRR12)	(0-6-0)	Baldwin #617
116.	John Springs	(4-4-0)	Baldwin #618
117.	Alex Black	(2-4-0)	Baldwin #619 (lost, 1861)

EXTENSION: THE NORTH EASTERN RAILROAD

To regain a railroad of its own, the city of Charleston chartered a new line through the state legislature. The North Eastern Railroad was chartered in December of 1851 to invade the territory of the Wilmington & Manchester and to connect with the Cheraw & Darlington. Surveys were completed for the NE in 1854, a year after the W&M opened its line to Manchester. Running due north from Charleston, the line only had to bridge the Santee River and a few small streams as it passed through Moncks Corner, St. Stephens, Kingstree and Lake City to Florence, which was on the W&M mainline.

EXTENSION: LAURENS RAILROAD

The Laurens Railroad was chartered in December of 1847 by the people of Laurens who had been bypassed by the Greenville & Columbia, which had turned westward at Newberry to run to Greenwood. This was the third of the county seat railroads on the Greenville & Columbia, but unlike the Abbeville and Anderson G&C branches, this was an independent operation. Shortly after the completion of the Greenville & Columbia, the Laurens Railroad was opened in 1854 running from Newberry directly to Laurens.

A SUMMATION OF THE FORTUNES OF THE SCRR

By 1855, the South Carolina Rail Road stretched from Charleston west to Augusta, Georgia, north to Columbia and northeast to Camden, with financially related lines extending on to Greenville and Charlotte. It had a friendly connection with the Georgia Rail Road, interchanging in Augusta to connect to lines that stretched to the Ohio River, a goal that had eluded Robert Y. Hayne. A semi-rival interchanged at Manchester while sharing the cost of the Camden Branch in an arrangement made with the Wilmington & Manchester in exchange for rights over the SCRR tracks into Columbia.

The convoluted financial reorganizations of the Charleston & Hamburg from 1827 to 1850 had wrestled control of the South Carolina Rail Road from the merchants of

Charleston, although the line continued to feed freight and produce into the port city for export and took away imported goods bound for the cities above the Fall Line. By 1850, the state was able to dictate the fortunes of the SCRR, the Greenville & Columbia and the Charlotte & South Carolina. Charleston had little say in the state's programs for internal improvement.

BAMBERG, SOUTH CAROLINA

Lowery's Turnout, west of Midway, was renamed Bamberg in 1855 when the new village was incorporated and named for Major William Sanborn Bamberg, who owned much of the land in the area.

LOCOMOTIVES OF 1855

Six locomotives were purchased in 1855, one from Rogers, Ketch and Grosvenor, two from Norris and three 4-4-0s from Baldwin. Much like the loss of the Alex Black (120), the Thomas Dotterer was also lost in 1861 when it disappeared.

118.	Thomas Rogers (SCRR17)		Ketch & Grosvenor
119.	H.W. Conner		Norris (sold to M&T, 1861)
120.	James Gadsden (SCRR18)	(4-4-0)	Baldwin #644
121.	Thomas Dotterer	(4-4-0)	Baldwin #660 (lost, 1861)
122.	G.B. Lythgoe (SCRR19)	(4-4-0)	Baldwin #662
123.	C.M. Furman (SCRR20)		Norris

EXTENSION: CHERAW & DARLINGTON

The Cheraw & Darlington line was opened to Cheraw in November of 1855 and relied entirely on the Wilmington & Manchester interchange in the first two years to get the goods to the port at Wilmington. In some cases, lumber and naval stores traveled west over the W&M to Kingville and then south over the South Carolina Rail Road to the port at Charleston. When the North Eastern Railroad was built from Charleston to Florence, the freight began to move directly to Charleston.

1856—RAILWAYS IN AMERICA

Railroad development was far spread across the nation, with some 20,000 miles of American railroads in operation versus the peak of 5,000 miles of the eastern canal

Built in 1857 by Baldwin, the Sam Tate, or SCRR #29, was photographed in 1880. The Sam Tate was the first locomotive on the road known to have a full cab for the crew. The low-capacity SCRR boxcar is typical of this period, with an arched roof and few safety appliances. This photo was owned by Mrs. B.E. Robinson of Charleston and was used as an illustration by the Southern Railway Company. *Courtesy of Southern Railway (Norfolk Southern).*

systems. The longest railway in the world in 1856 was the Illinois Central, which operated over a mainline of 784 miles and connected Chicago to New Orleans. The thirty-two states and the nine territories at that time had a population of 27 million, of which 23 million were recent European immigrants.

LOCOMOTIVES OF 1856

Nine locomotives were purchased in 1856, a purchase indicative of the prosperity of the South Carolina Rail Road at that time. Amazingly, the Thomas C. Perrin, a Baldwin 4-4-0, disappeared in 1861.

124.	William C. Dukes (SCRR21)		RK&G
125.	Henry Gourdin (SCRR22)		RK&G
126.	L.J. Patterson (SCRR23)		RK&G
127.	John Bryce (SCRR24)	(4-4-0)	Baldwin #678
128.	James Rose (SCRR25)	(4-4-0)	Baldwin #686
129.	T. Tupper 2 (SCRR26)		Norris
130.	George A. Trenholm (SCRR27)		Norris
131.	Thomas C. Perrin	(4-4-0)	Baldwin 713 (lost, 1861)
132.	Governor Adams (SCRR28)	(4-4-0)	Baldwin #724

Locomotives with Crew Cabs

It is not easy to determine when the first locomotive on the South Carolina Rail Road was equipped with an all-weather cab to protect the crew. One possibility is the Rough & Ready, built by Ross Winans in 1847 for the company. A sister locomotive, Juno, built for the Baltimore & Ohio, was rebuilt in 1856 with a conventional cab to cover the locomotive engineer and fireman positions, and the idea may have been transferred to the SCRR.

The first SCRR locomotive positively identified with a cab was the Sam Tate, a 4-4-0 American class built by Baldwin as its #742 in February 1857. This became SC#29 in service when the road phased out the use of names for locomotives.

LOCOMOTIVES OF 1857

133.	Sam Tate (SCRR29)	(4-4-0)	Baldwin #742
134.	Preston S. Brooks (SCRR30)		Norris
135.	L.M. Keitt (SCRR31)		RK&G

EXTENSION: THE NORTH EASTERN RAILROAD

The North Eastern Railroad line was completed in 1857 and the company quickly built a track connection to the Cheraw & Darlington, creating a through line to Cheraw. With this line in place, lumber and naval stores were shipped directly to the port at Charleston, which paid back the support of the merchants there.

THE 4-6-0 TEN-WHEELER DESIGN

In both 1858 and 1859, a 4-6-0 freight locomotive was included in the orders for new Baldwin steam engines. SCRR#33 weighed twenty-seven tons and had forty-eight-inch drivers for greater adhesion. Based on a design that fulfilled the specifications of J. Edgar Thomson, once of the Georgia Rail Road and at that time president of the Pennsylvania Railroad Company, the performance of this new design made the 4-6-0 ten-wheeler Baldwin Locomotive Works' standard freight locomotive for years to come.

LOCOMOTIVES OF 1858

The company again held purchases down to three locomotives in 1858, buying two Baldwins and a Rogers.

The James S. Corry, or SCRR #40, is seen at Baldwin Locomotive Works at Eddystone, Pennsylvania, near Philadelphia in 1859, just before shipment to South Carolina. This twenty-three-ton locomotive had fifty-inch drivers and an outside frame supported by long diagonal braces. It is resting on strap rail timber track kept in gauge with tie rods. *Author's collection.*

136.	William P. Miles (SCRR32)	(4-4-0)	Baldwin #798 (renamed S. Miles)
137.	M.W. Baldwin (SCRR33)	(4-6-0)	Baldwin #803
138.	James S. Scott (SCRR34)		RK&G

SCRR LOCOMOTIVE #40

The James S. Corry, SCRR #40, was built by Baldwin (#905) in December of 1859 as a 4-6-0, the sixth of this wheel arrangement that the SCRR purchased for freight service. It also had a full cab, but a more elaborate one with more windows. The J.S. Corry came with a Radley & Hunter "smoke pipe" and unusual outside frames. The tender was forty-two inches deep and could hold eighteen hundred gallons of water.

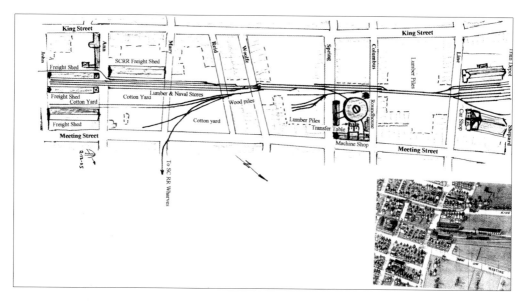

The shops of the South Carolina Rail Road at Charleston were built in the narrow block between King Street and Meeting Street south of Line Street. The completely circular roundhouse at Columbus had tracks leading to a transfer table that placed cars in the machine shop on Meeting. The 1852 freight shed was just north of Ann Street, while the two warehouses known as Camden Depot were on either side of three tracks south of Ann. The freight shed to the right later was remodeled to become the Charleston Visitor Center in the last years of the twentieth century. *Map by author.*

Locomotives of 1859

The need for more of the standard Baldwin freight locomotive prompted the South Carolina Rail Road to buy seven of them in 1859 after one year of testing the merits of the M.W. Baldwin.

139. Thomas Waring (SCRR35)   (4-6-0)   Baldwin #837

140. W.C. Gatewood (SCRR36)   (4-6-0)   Baldwin #850

141. A. Burnside (SCRR37)   (4-6-0)   Baldwin #852

142. E.F. Raworth (SCRR38)   (4-6-0)   Baldwin #855

143. C.T. Mitchell (SCRR39)   (4-6-0)   Baldwin #861

144. J.S. Corry (SCRR40)   (4-6-0)   Baldwin #905

145. W.S. Stockman (SCRR41)   (4-6-0)   Baldwin #901

The City Council Census of 1861

The Charleston City Council Census of 1861 reveals some other structures associated with the South Carolina Rail Road Company. Slaves belonging to the SCRR were housed at 31 Columbus Street, 2½ Hanover Street and 26 John Street, all of which

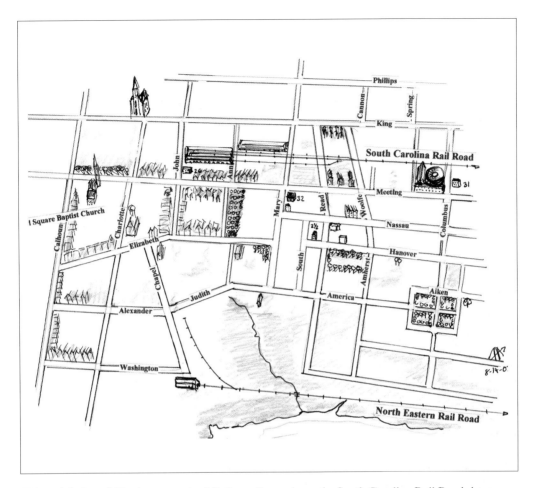

This aerial view of Charleston north of Calhoun Street shows the South Carolina Rail Road slave quarters, as called out in the City Council Census of 1861. All of the structures were on SCRR property or no more than two blocks east of Meeting Street. *Map by author.*

were wooden houses. Meeting Street had two wooden houses at 257 and 259 on the west side of the street that were also used to house slaves belonging to the company. Across the street at 243 was a third wooden house used for the same purpose. Just at the end of the block at 223 Meeting on the east side was the brick firehouse of the Eagle Engine Company, one of a number of volunteer fire companies in town. John Street, which runs west from Elizabeth to King just above Chapel Street, had a brick storage building at 22 on the north side and a wooden storage building at 24. A block north, Mary Street, which runs from America Street to King Street, had the offices of the South Carolina Rail Road Company at 32, a wooden building on the north side of the street. Romney Street, located on the Charleston Neck, ran from Meeting Street, below the Forks of the Road, to King Street, nearly opposite Simons Street. This very short street had a brick house for slaves on the south side at 1 and was owned by the South Carolina Rail Road farm nearby. Across the street at 2 and 4 were two wooden

This 1860 map of South Carolina shows the rail system that had developed in the preceding decade. Only two Georgia cities offer rail transit to the state's interior, while North Carolina has three lines entering the state headed for Wilmington on the coast, Rockingham (south of Raleigh) and Charlotte in the Piedmont area. *Author's collection.*

houses owned by Joseph Noisette, a free person of color. Noisette lived at 2 and John Edwards, also a free person of color, lived at 4. Noisette owned the Noisette Farm on the Charleston Neck.

EXTENSION: SPARTANBURG & UNION RAILWAY

Some eleven years after being chartered and with three state loans required to finance the job, the Spartanburg & Union completed its line through to Alston on the Greenville & Columbia and became, unwittingly, a partner of the larger line.

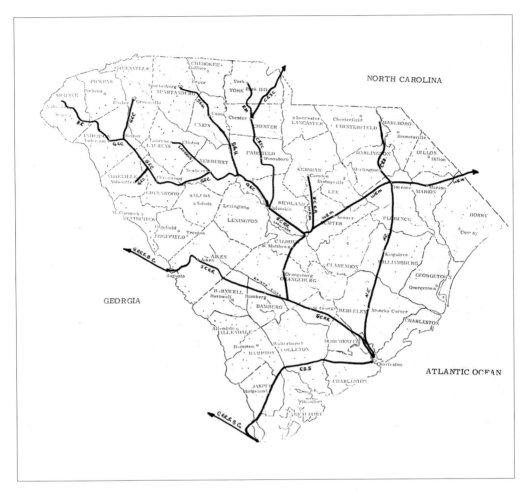

The 1860 railroad map of South Carolina identifies each line and the general area served. Note the number of courthouse branch lines that have been built as these towns begin to see the benefits of rail transportation. *Map by author.*

EXTENSION: THE CHARLESTON & SAVANNAH RAILROAD

After four years of struggling to push its rail line through the marshy waters of the coast, the Charleston & Savannah reached Georgia after completing a major bridge across the Savannah River. Completed in October 1860, the railroad had only six months of prosperity until the great conflict was to begin.

Although the C&S entered Savannah over the tracks of the Central Railroad & Banking Company, making a connection at Central Junction northwest of the city, the railroad did not enter the city of Charleston because of the Ashley River, a wide tidal stream. The tracks ended in Saint Andrews Parish and all freight had to be teamed across the river in wagons.

THE SOUTH CAROLINA RAIL NETWORK IN 1860

Here then was the network of rails at the raising of the curtain on the Civil War. From Charleston, rails ran north through Florence to Cheraw, west and south to Savannah and west to Augusta, Columbia and Cheraw. From Columbia, the rails continued on, running east to Wilmington, North Carolina, north to Charlotte, and northwest to Walhalla, Greenville, Laurens, Spartanburg and Yorkville. The war was to completely destroy two of these lines and severely damage and cripple the progress and growth of the remainder.

LOCOMOTIVES OF 1860

The company bought three new Baldwin 4-4-0s and a used 1850 Portland Company locomotive from the Spartanburg & Union in 1860. The new Baldwin #902 was originally known as W. Pettit but was renamed J.A. Allen for no known reason. This machine also disappeared in 1861 with no explanation.

146.	W. Pettit	(4-4-0)	Baldwin #902 (renamed J.A. Allen; lost 1861)
147.	no name (SCRR42)		Portland Co. (formerly S&U)
148.	General James Simon (SCRR43)	(4-4-0)	Baldwin #933
149.	W.D. Porter (SCRR44)	(4-4-0)	Baldwin #937

The War Between the States

The Southern states formed the new Confederate States of America in Montgomery, Alabama, on February 9, 1861, with Jefferson Davis as the new president pro tem until elections could be held. These seven states were South Carolina, Mississippi, Florida, Alabama, Georgia, Louisiana and Texas, listed in the order of their secession from the Union.

Abraham Lincoln was sworn in as president on March 4, 1861, less than a month later. South Carolina had wanted Federal troops to leave Fort Sumter at the mouth of Charleston Harbor in January and negotiated with the commandant. President Buchanan had sent the *Star of the West* to the fort to resupply the position, but the South Carolina forces fired at the ship to make it retreat. With no way to replenish the supplies, an agreement was made for the Federal forces to leave the fort on April 12. However, the troops did not move and the first shots of the war were fired at Fort Sumter on April 12, 1861. Lincoln then called for the Northern states to send troops to recapture Fort Sumter and other forts that had been taken. This call by Lincoln for troops to be sent from all states led the remaining Southern states to resist by seceding from the Union.

Virginia joined the CSA five days later and was joined by Arkansas and North Carolina in May and by Tennessee in June. The capital was moved to Richmond, Virginia, on May 29. The CSA also claimed control over Indian Territory (Oklahoma) and Arizona Territory extending from Texas to California.

The largest city in the new CSA was New Orleans with a population of 169,000, the sixth largest in the United States. Charleston with 41,000 was second in the CSA and twenty-second in the United States. Richmond was third in the CSA with 38,000 and twenty-fifth in the country. However, New Orleans was retaken by the Union forces in 1862, leaving Charleston and Richmond as the two largest cities in the CSA for the duration of the war.

The War Between the States had little effect on the South Carolina Rail Road during the first three years of the conflict. The port city of Charleston was under occasional Federal bombardment from Fort Sumter, which was back in Union hands after the first months, as well as from blockade ships. But the rail terminals, north of Calhoun Street and far from the Battery at the foot of the peninsula, suffered little damage. The railroad lines in South Carolina carried large numbers of troops and great amounts of war material, including artillery and shells.

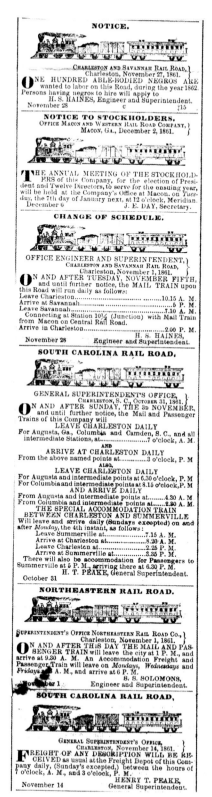

NOTICE.

CHARLESTON AND SAVANNAH RAIL ROAD,
Charleston, November 27, 1861.

ONE HUNDRED ABLE-BODIED NEGROS ARE
wanted to labor on this Road, during the year 1862.
Persons having negros to hire will apply to
H. S. HAINES, Engineer and Superintendent.
November 28   c   †15

NOTICE TO STOCKHOLDERS.
OFFICE MACON AND WESTERN RAIL ROAD COMPANY,
MACON, GA., December 2, 1861.

THE ANNUAL MEETING OF THE STOCKHOLD-
ERS of this Company, for the election of President and Twelve Directors, to serve for the ensuing year,
will be held at the Company's Office at Macon. on Tuesday, the 7th day of January next, at 12 o'clock, Meridian.
December 6   J. E. DAY, Secretary.

CHANGE OF SCHEDULE.

OFFICE ENGINEER AND SUPERINTENDENT,
CHARLESTON AND SAVANNAH RAIL ROAD,
Charleston, November 1, 1861.

ON AND AFTER TUESDAY, NOVEMBER FIFTH,
and until further notice, the MAIL TRAIN upon
this Road will run daily as follows:
Leave Charleston.................................10.15 A. M.
Arrive at Savannah..................................5 P. M.
Leave Savannah....................................7.10 A. M.
Connecting at Station 10½ (Junction) with Mail Train
from Macon on Central Rail Road.
Arrive in Charleston...............................2.00 P. M.
H. S. HAINES,
November 28   Engineer and Superintendent.

SOUTH CAROLINA RAIL ROAD,

GENERAL SUPERINTENDENT'S OFFICE,
CHARLESTON, S. C., OCTOBER 31, 1861.

ON AND AFTER SUNDAY, THE 3D NOVEMBER,
and until further notice, the Mail and Passenger
Trains of this Company will
LEAVE CHARLESTON DAILY
For Augusta, Ga., Columbia and Camden, S. C., and all
intermediate Stations, at.......................7 o'clock, A. M.
AND
ARRIVE AT CHARLESTON DAILY
From the above named points at..............3 o'clock, P. M
ALSO,
LEAVE CHARLESTON DAILY
For Augusta and intermediate points at 6.30 o'clock, P. M
For Columbia and intermediate points at 8.15 o'clock, P. M
AND ARRIVE DAILY
From Augusta and intermediate points at........4.30 A. M
From Columbia and intermediate points at......2.30 A. M.
THE SPECIAL ACCOMMODATION TRAIN
BETWEEN CHARLESTON AND SUMMERVILLE
Will leave and arrive daily (Sundays excepted) on and
after Monday, the 4th instant, as follows:
Leave Summerville at...................7.15 A. M.
Arrive at Charleston at..................8.20 A. M.
Leave Charleston at......................2.25 P. M.
Arrive at Summerville at................3.35 P. M.
There will also be accommodation for Passengers to
Summerville at 5 P. M., arriving there at 6.30 P. M.
H. T. PEAKE, General Superintendent.
October 31

NORTHEASTERN RAIL ROAD.

SUPERINTENDENT'S OFFICE NORTHEASTERN RAIL ROAD Co.,
Charleston, November 1, 1861.

ON AND AFTER THIS DAY THE MAIL AND PAS-
SENGER TRAIN will leave the city at 1 P. M., and
arrive at 9.30 A. M. An Accommodation Freight and
Passenger Train will leave on Mondays, Wednesdays and
Fridays at 8 A. M., and arrive at 6 P. M.
S. S. SOLOMONS,
November 1   Engineer and Superintendent.

SOUTH CAROLINA RAIL ROAD,

GENERAL SUPERINTENDENT'S OFFICE,
CHARLESTON, November 14, 1861.

FREIGHT OF ANY DESCRIPTION WILL BE RE-
CEIVED as usual at the Freight Depot of this Com-
pany daily, (Sunday's excepted,) between the hours of
7 o'clock, A. M., and 3 o'clock, P. M.
HENRY T. PEAKE,
November 14   General Superintendent.

This 1861 broadleaf shows the scheduled trains leaving
Charleston as of December 26, 1861. *Collection of David
Carriker.*

THE TWO CONFEDERATE RAILROAD ACTS OF 1861

The Confederate government that dictated the rail's fortune during the war considered the connection by rail of the Charleston & Savannah with the South Carolina Rail Road and the North Eastern Railroad to be essential for the effective transfer of military movements of men and material. An act authorizing the construction of a railroad bridge across the Ashley River at Charleston was passed in 1861.

Another act had quite the opposite effect on the Laurens Railroad. It was determined that this short courthouse line was of no value and that its rails would be of more use in building a connection between two isolated lines in North Carolina. The Laurens was confiscated in 1862 and the rails were pulled up and shipped to Greensboro to be used on the new Piedmont Railroad, which ran north to Danville, Virginia. The Laurens right-of-way lay abandoned for thirteen years until the track was replaced by the Greenville and Columbia line.

DEFENDING THE C&S

The Charleston & Savannah was the only line to be in danger of direct attack throughout the war, and indeed it suffered from attacks nearly every month after November. Early in the war, the South Carolina Rail Road loaned a number of boxcars to the C&S for moving essential military equipment and troops, but within a year was forced to recall the equipment as shipments began to increase on their line.

The Federal forces captured Hilton Head Island near Port Royal, about two-thirds of the distance from Charleston to Savannah, in November of 1861. They used this as the base of their naval operations. The CSA placed a heavy guard along the right-of-way at the bridges since the Federal forces were confined to using shallow-draft naval boats to navigate the streams in the swamps. Robert E. Lee was assigned as commanding general at Coosawhatchie in December of 1861 and led the CSA in beating off the major attacks aimed at the C&S in the spring and fall of 1862.

In 1863, only minor attacks and sorties continued to place a thorn in the C&S Railway's operations. But the bottleneck at Charleston was relieved with the completion of the railway bridge. The bridge that opened in April of 1864 was built with rails to move equipment to the city, but there was no turntable on the Charleston side of the Ashley River. The company had the trains back across the bridge to reach Charleston and return running forward to get trains back to west of the Ashley. This created the essential link in the rail network of the Confederacy as the South Carolina, the North Eastern and the Charleston & Savannah were all directly connected by rail. However, teams were usually used to move the cars from the bridge end to the two other lines, as Charleston ordinances prohibited the operation of steam locomotives on the streets.

Some trains of the Charleston & Savannah cars ran on to Florence over the North Eastern and in some cases on to the port of Wilmington, North Carolina. This caused great problems for the little line that complained to Richmond of the loss of equipment when the cars and locomotives were not sent back to South Carolina.

The next year, the Union began to mount more serious attacks and one major attack took place in May of 1864. Some two thousand men under General Birney sought to destroy the Edisto River bridges. Through an error, the Yankees ran aground in the shallow estuarial waters and were forced to abandon the attack under the direct fire of a Confederate battery that burned the army transport *Boston* to the waterline. In November, a force of five hundred men attacked the C&S near Grahamville, but was beaten off by a unit of the Georgia militia. In early December, another massive strike was made up the Coosawhatchie and the Pocataligo Rivers to the C&S Railroad bridges there, but once more was unsuccessful.

The Confederate army established a prisoner of war camp just north of Columbia in 1864 that was unofficially known as Camp Sorghum after the sorghum molasses that formed a basic part of the prisoners' daily ration. In October of 1864, some 1,500 Union prisoners were carried by rail from Charleston over the South Carolina Rail Road when a threat of a yellow fever epidemic arose in the Lowcountry. About 150 Yankees managed to escape from the slow-moving train in the Carolina swamps during the journey to Columbia. Those who remained on the train found an empty field instead of an organized camp. They were forced to build their own shelter from limbs of trees, blankets and old bed ticks taken from Charleston's Roper Hospital.

Riding the Trains from Atlanta to Richmond — Summer 1863

A lieutenant colonel in the British army made a three-month tour of the CSA from April to June of 1863. Arthur Fremantle entered the country near Brownsville, coming up from Mexico, and traveled north and east to Richmond, Virginia. His book, *Three Months in the Southern States*, is recommended reading.

On June 5, he arrived in Atlanta from Chattanooga on the Western & Atlantic. He found the train very crowded with "wounded and sick soldiers returning on leave to their homes." He arrived at 3:00 a.m. on Saturday, June 6. The next train he used traveled on the Georgia Railroad and covered 174 miles.

> *After breakfasting, I started again for Augusta at 7 PM. The train had not proceeded ten miles before it was brought up by an obstruction, in the shape of a broken down freight train, one of whose cars was completely smashed. This delayed us for about an hour, but we made up for it afterwards and arrived at Augusta at 5:15 PM. At some of the stations, provisions for the soldiers were brought into the cars by ladies and distributed gratis. When I refused on the ground of not being a soldier, these ladies looked at me with great suspicion, mingled with contempt, and as their looks evidently expressed the words "then why are you not a soldier?", I was obliged to explain to them who I was, and show them General Bragg's pass which astonished them not a little. I was told that Georgia was the only state in which soldiers were still so liberally treated. They have become so common everywhere else.*
>
> *I left Augusta on Sunday at 7 PM by train for Charleston. My car was much crowded with Yankee prisoners.* [They may have been bound for Camp Sorghum north of Columbia.]

Very likely from *Harper's Weekly* or a similar publication, this drawing illustrates the escape of several Yankee prisoners who are darting into the Congaree River Swamp as armed guards seem more intent on where the train is headed. *Collection of Mrs. Fenton.*

I arrived at Charleston at 5 AM on Monday. I left Charleston by rail at 2 PM. I declined traveling in the ladies car although offered that privilege. The advantage of a small amount of extra cleanliness being outweighed by the screaming of the children and the constant liability of being turned out of one's place for a female. We arrived at Florence at 9 PM where we were detained for some time owing to a break-down of another train. We then fought our way into some desperately crowded cars [on the Wilmington & Manchester] *and continued our journey throughout the night.*

Arrived at Wilmington at 5 AM and crossed the river there in a steamer. I was obliged to go to the Provost Marshall's office to get Beauregard's pass renewed there, as North Carolina is out of his district. In doing so, I very nearly missed the train.

I left Wilmington at 7 AM [using the Wilmington & Weldon on June 16]. *The weather was very hot and oppressive, and the cars were dreadfully crowded all day. The luxuries of Charleston had also spoiled me for the "road" as I could no longer appreciate at their proper value the "hog and hominy" meals which I had been so thankful for in Texas. We changed cars again at Weldon* [to the Petersburg Railroad] *where I had a terrific fight for a seat, but I succeeded, for experience had made me very quick at this sort of business. I always carry my saddlebags and knapsack with me into the car.*

We reached Petersburg at 3 AM and had to get out and traverse this town in carts after which we had to lie down in the road until some other cars were opened. [Fremantle probably means that many of the passengers lay down on the railroad in front of the locomotive until additional cars were attached.] *We left Petersburg at 5 AM and arrived at Richmond at 7 AM having taken forty one hours coming from Charleston. The railroad between Petersburg and Richmond is protected by extensive field works and the woods have been cut down to give range. An irruption of the enemy in this direction has been contemplated.*

Fremantle's trip can be evaluated in another way to judge the railroad conditions. His trip over the Western & Atlantic was made at thirteen miles per hour; the Georgia Rail Road at nineteen miles per hour (not counting the lost hour); the South Carolina Rail Road at fourteen miles per hour; and the North Eastern at four and a half miles per hour. His comments allow us to visualize just how difficult travel was in mid-1863, yet he traveled with a military pass to assure better treatment.

RESTRICTIONS ON DAILY TRAINS—EARLY 1864

The quartermaster general office at Richmond sent a telegram on March 26, 1864, to Major General W.H. Whiting at Wilmington to complain about the number of regular passenger trains on the Wilmington & Manchester.

I regret to learn that the Manchester & Wilmington [sic] *Road are running two daily passenger trains. This is complained of by the South Carolina Road which is restricted to one, and whose cars are detained at Kingville on account of the failure of the W&M to remove freight as soon as delivered. The order was positive that only one train should run on any Road between Richmond and Augusta.*

A.R. Lawton

Clearly the army wished the railroads to be clear of regular daily trains to allow for the passage of freight trains and special military movements over the same lines. Blocking of the South Carolina rails at Kingville and preventing passage of their trains was equally upsetting.

N.J. BELL'S ADVENTURES ON THE SOUTH CAROLINA RAIL ROAD

Conductor N.J. Bell had worked for the Western & Atlantic operating trains between Atlanta and Chattanooga, or to Dalton, Georgia, where the line met the East Tennessee & Georgia line. After being falsely accused of wrecking a train, he managed to get the

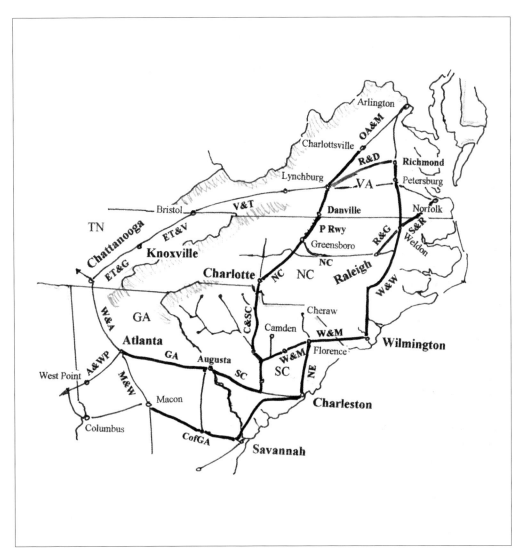

A map of the principal rail routes from Atlanta and Macon in Georgia to Wilmington on the coast in North Carolina, Charlotte and via other lines to Richmond in Virginia. Note the Piedmont Railway between Greensboro and Danville that used the rails of the Laurens Railroad in South Carolina. *Map by author.*

case straightened out and then quit to join the ET&G. Based out of Dalton, he mostly operated up to Knoxville, but as the war progressed, there were fewer and fewer tracks available until the company destroyed the remaining equipment at Loudon, Tennessee, south of Knoxville. Bell then walked to Bristol, Tennessee, and caught a train to Petersburg, then south to Weldon, on to Wilmington, then to Kingville, Branchville and Augusta to finally reach home near Atlanta.

He moved his family to Covington east of Atlanta and then went to Augusta. Here he again began to work for the East Tennessee & Georgia using locomotives and freight and passenger cars of that line and running across South Carolina to either Charlotte or to Wilmington, North Carolina, on the coast. His story is the subject of *Southern Railroad Man*, edited by James A Ward, who gave permission to relate some of the South Carolina adventures.

It seems extraordinary that trains of the ET&G, a railroad that had been destroyed by Union forces skirmishing between Knoxville and Chattanooga, could be operating freely from Augusta to Wilmington over the South Carolina railroads, yet the cost of shipping on an ET&G train was certainly not free. Cotton was shipped east to run the blockade out of Wilmington and reach Nassau. Here European goods were purchased, crossed back through the naval blockade and traveled by ET&G trains back to Augusta. Shippers paid twice: a freight fee to the ET&G for the use of the train and another freight fee for transit over the SCRR and the Wilmington & Manchester Railroad.

Bell tells us,

> *Soon after I arrived at Augusta, I was fitted up with an East Tennessee & Georgia second class coach for my caboose. This coach was supplied with a cook stove and most of the seats were taken out and good beds put up to sleep on. These were arranged so that they could be turned back out of the way when not in use. This car was a combination car, one end having been used for baggage or express.*
>
> *We were required to have a pilot on each road that we ran over—a conductor who would take charge of the running of the train—but somehow it happened that I ran some trips without any pilot. As soon as everything was ready, and I had bought my rations, I left Augusta for Wilmington, NC with a train load of cotton. The roads we ran over would not allow us to run after dark, so we would side track about sundown and sometimes before. I had an engineer, fireman, and a wood-passer. There was also a brakeman and a cook. The company paid for our rations.*
>
> *I made one or two trips to Charlotte (using the SCRR to Columbia and the Charlotte & South Carolina to reach Charlotte). Sometimes I would make a trip over the Georgia Railroad and get a trainload of cotton.*
>
> *Sometimes it would take a week to unload and reload a train at Wilmington and we would lay over there. Sometimes the yard at Wilmington would get blocked and we would have to side-track about twelve miles out on the road and stay two or three days before we could get in.*
>
> *The first alligator I ever saw was by the side of the track on the South Carolina Rail Road. It had been killed by a train. In that same section I saw my first cypress swamps and rice plantations.*
>
> *Some of the bridges and trestles were very shackly [shaky] that we ran over between Augusta and Wilmington. I have noticed trestles in passing over them and while the weight of the engine and train were upon them the bents would go down with the mudsills out of sight in the mud, and as the train passed off, rise up again. I did not like it at first, but soon got used to it.*
>
> *The land was sandy, piney woods, cypress swamps, small lakes, rice plantations, and bull frogs innumerable which kept up such a noise at night that I could sleep but little until*

I got more used to them. Snakes were so plentiful through the swamps in warm weather that I was afraid to step off my train along the roadside. I have actually seen two or three at a time, and heard more crawling through the grass.

I saw one belt of pine woods where the ground was covered with sand as white as snow and the first time I saw it I thought it was sure enough snow. Toward Wilmington, there was a great deal of piney woods and there were many turpentine stills. There were nice lakes along the roadside in North Carolina. I could not see how anyone could make a living in that section of the country, for it was very poor land and thinly settled.

I avoided a bad wreck on the road one morning after lying all night on a side track as we were not allowed to run after dark. The freight conductor who had charge of the train set the switch to the side track (they called them gates, though, on that road), and after he did so, he motioned the engineer ahead, and before I could get to the engine, the engineer had started. I stopped him and ran ahead to the switch and asked the pilot what it meant. He said that he wanted to go. I said that there was a passenger train due there in ten minutes and he said that it had already passed. I replied that it had not; that it was an extra that had passed by and the regular train was not due when that train passed us. I had not more that got him to set the switch to the main track before here came the regular passenger train at as fast a rate of speed as they ran in those days.

When I was running on the South Carolina road, it did not make any difference how many sections of trains there were on one schedule, there were no signals carried on engines to give notice of a train following, but the conductor of the front train would hold up as many fingers as there were trains following him on the same schedule. When he met a train going in the opposite direction, for instance, there were five trains on one schedule, the front conductor would hold up 4 fingers; the second conductor would hold up 3 fingers; the third conductor would hold up two fingers and the fourth conductor would hold up one finger. So we had to look out for fingers when meeting trains. All such rules were new to me, but I soon became familiar with them after I commenced running over these roads.

There were one or two engineers who were employed by the East Tennessee & Georgia Railroad Company who left their engines standing in the yard at Wilmington and went on some of the vessels that were running the blockade between Wilmington and Nassau, and other engineers had to be sent from Augusta to take charge of the engines that were thus left standing in the yard.

Bell was an experienced conductor who knew the rules of his home roads and was quick to adapt to the rules of the roads he shepherded his trains over to reach the coast. Considering the regular trains, the military trains and the special foreign road trains, it is a wonder that there were not far more accidents and disasters in this period.

The Flight of the Western & Atlantic Train

General Sherman was on his way to Atlanta. Everyone was aware of this, but there was uncertainty as to what Sherman and his Union troops would do to the city and to the railroads. The governor of Georgia, Joseph E. Brown, gave Jim Mullins and John Chester a dangerous assignment late in 1864. Governor Brown had already commandeered the Western & Atlantic Shops in Atlanta to protect the valuable assets of the railroad that connected Atlanta to Chattanooga in Tennessee. He knew that the northern end of the W&A was already in the hands of the Yankees. In addition, the Atlanta & West Point had been torn up to the southwest and the Georgia Rail Road had fallen to the enemy at Decatur, five miles to the east. The only safe route out of town was over the track of the Macon & Western.

But when Governor Brown heard that the Confederates had been beaten near Jonesboro on the Macon & Western, he was spurred into action. He told Jim Mullins, master mechanic of the W&A, to "pick the best engine you've got and hitch on as many dead locomotives as she can haul, load the shop machinery into the cars and get the whole shebang to hell out of town."

Mullins picked John Chester, who had worked for the Western & Atlantic since the early 1850s, to be the engineer and Joe Crofts to be conductor for the special train and told Chester to assemble it and load the crew's families as quickly as possible to leave that very day. Although Chester wanted to use the General, which had been stolen in 1862 by twenty-two Yankee spies in the daring Andrews Raid, Dave Young, the General's assigned engineer, would not part with it and the Missouri was picked as the replacement. Both the General and the Missouri had been the last two locomotives to be delivered to the W&A before the war began and thus were the most valuable to the company.

The train as put together by John Chester consisted of the Missouri, six dead locomotives, two boxcars to hold Chester and Croft's families with a few furnishings and all the food they could find, plus four boxcars loaded with drill presses and lathes from the W&A Atlanta shops.

The elusive train headed southwest toward Palmetto, Georgia, twenty-four miles out, using the Atlanta & West Point tracks, and when it reached Palmetto it laid over for refueling. That night it continued west to Opelika, Alabama. There it switched onto the tracks of the Southwestern Railroad and began a return back to Georgia. Heading eastward to Columbus, Georgia, the train passed through town fairly quickly, stopping only for fuel and water, and then rolled east. The next day, the train continued its trek for one hundred miles to Macon and the safety of the tracks of the Macon & Western.

Atlanta fell to Sherman's troops that same day. But a telegraphic message gave the crew orders on November 16 to run the refugee train down the Central of Georgia tracks to Grissold. Arriving at this small village, it lay hidden from Sherman's forces on the CofGA mainline back in the woods.

Word came a day or two later to move the train once more. Chester was ready and after getting everyone aboard, the train rolled on southeast over the CofGA to Savannah. It then proceeded to Central Junction, where it passed onto the tracks of the Charleston & Savannah and into South Carolina using the trestles and drawbridge. The train then crawled past the stoutly defended bridges and stations along the C&S for 108 miles to Charleston as Sherman's men marched into Savannah not long after, on December 18.

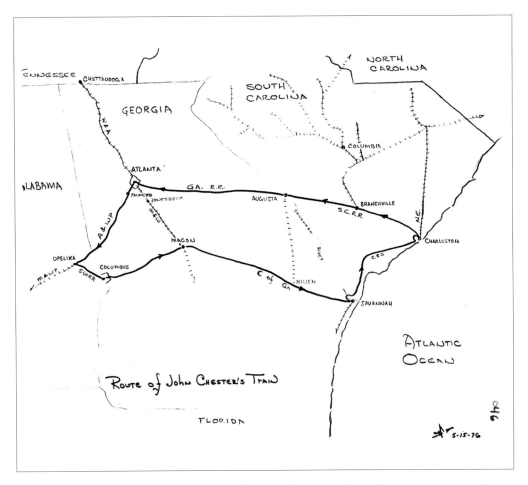

The route of John Chester on the Western & Atlantic train sent out from Atlanta to protect several locomotives, and the railroad machinery form the company shops. This was likely the longest trip by any refugee train that occurred during the last months of the war. *Map by author.*

Chester figured Sherman would plan to work north along the Savannah & Augusta RR in an effort to crush the second largest city in Georgia, and he would be safe in Charleston. But Sherman had other ideas. In a week or so, word came that the Federal troops had crossed the Savannah and they were following the coast to Charleston following the C&S tracks, destroying the rails and buildings along the way.

Getting up steam once more, the beleaguered train crossed the Ashley River over the new CSA bridge that connected the C&S to the SCRR and the North Eastern. Here the train was put on the rails of the South Carolina Rail Road and headed out of town toward Summerville. Chester followed the tracks past Branchville to Augusta, narrowly missing one of several bands of Sherman's men, who tore up the Augusta line from Aiken to the Edisto River just hours after they had passed by.

Arriving safely in Augusta after crossing the Savannah River, Chester persuaded Johnny Cook, master mechanic of the Georgia Rail Road, to overhaul one of the dead engines that had developed bearing trouble. On April 9, 1865, the surrender of General Lee ended the dreams of the CSA.

Chester was anxious to return home to Atlanta, but the sixty miles of torn-up Georgia road between Social Circle and Atlanta prevented any thought of travel. The track was later replaced under U.S. Military Railroad supervision and when complete, the little refugee train, with John Chester and Jim Mullins, their families, seven locomotives and four cars of machine presses and tooling, steamed the 174 miles back to Atlanta to end the 700-mile flight from Atlanta.

This was but one of several trains commissioned by Governor Brown and of the engines and cars and equipment sent out, not a single piece was lost to enemy action.

SHERMAN'S FORCES MOVE TO SOUTH CAROLINA

General Sherman had begun his March to the Sea from the burned and recovered city of Atlanta in November of 1864 and entered the subdued Savannah on December 21, after cutting a swath through Georgia that severed the Confederacy's lines of communication and transportation. General Beauregard of the CSA set the Savannah River C&S bridgework to the torch on December 20 to stop any northward movement contemplated by Sherman's forces.

In February 1865, Sherman divided his forces and sent one half along the Charleston & Savannah toward Charleston and the second half northward toward Columbia, the state capital. The entire Charleston & Savannah was destroyed with the ties burned, rails melted and twisted out of shape and all stations and any equipment accidentally left behind put to the torch. General Grant asked Sherman, "What's to prevent their laying the rails again?" Sherman smirked and told him, "Why my bummers don't do things by halves. Every rail having been placed over a hot fire has been twisted as crooked as a ram's horn and they can never be used again." Unfortunately, this was true and the rails were never used again.

Charleston fell on February 18, 1865, and with it came the effective total abandonment of the Charleston & Savannah, which retained a partial roadbed and the franchises permitting operation. The South Carolina Rail Road was, of course, a primary target for the troops as they entered Charleston. But, forewarned, the SCRR had sent its engines and cars northward over the North Eastern and the Cheraw & Darlington to protect them from Sherman's savages.

On February 7, the northbound troops crossed the SCRR at the town of Midway, just west of Branchville. The track and the right-of-way were subjected to mass destruction as the Yankee troops burned the Edisto River Bridge east of Midway, effectively cutting the railroad line into two parts. The troops then worked their way westward toward Augusta, destroying track and property until they reached Windsor. Reforming at this point, they marched under orders back across the Lowcountry to Orangeburg on the branch to Columbia. Here they began a destruction of the South Carolina Rail Road line to Columbia, burning the Congaree and the Wateree River bridges as they passed.

Pocataligo Depot on the Charleston & Savannah Railroad after the troops had ripped up the rails and hoisted the Stars and Stripes. Harper's Weekly, *author's collection.*

General Sherman's "Bummers" methodically take apart the tracks of the Charleston & Savannah Railroad near Pocataligo, South Carolina, in March of 1865. The rails were placed over bonfires and twisted out of shape, the telegraph wires were cut and destroyed and the ties were burned. Harper's Weekly, *author's collection.*

A *Harper's Weekly* artist produced this illustration of the Fifteenth Corps crossing the South Edisto River for the Saturday, April 18, 1865 edition. The Federal troops of Sherman's army included several six-mule teams to pull supply wagons across the pontoon bridge built using wooden boats. Harper's Weekly, *author's collection.*

THE DIARY ENTRIES OF YANKEE TROOPS

Sherman's march through South Carolina was vividly described in day-to-day accounts in a diary kept by one of the men on the march. The force was divided at Savannah into a right and left contingent and each marched toward Columbia over a different route.

The left contingent marched north along the Savannah River, leaving Savannah on January 20, and attempted to cross the river at Sister's Ferry, hampered by wet ground and bad weather over a nine-day period from January 27 to February 4. On February 5, the troops marched through Brighton, South Carolina. In rapid succession, the forces captured and burned Lawtonville on February 7, Allendale on February 9 and Barnwell on February 10. Near Aiken, one squad had a firefight with a Confederate force as it was intent on destroying the mainline of the South Carolina Rail Road. The Yankees tore up ten miles of SCRR track near White Pond and then crossed the South Edisto River on February 13 and the North Edisto River on February 14. They then skirmished at Lexington and began to burn the town on February 16. The left contingent crossed the Broad River on February 17 and destroyed the tracks of the Greenville & Columbia Railroad and the Spartanburg & Alston Railroad at the Broad River Bridge at Alston, South Carolina.

The force then joined the right contingent at Winnsboro on February 21 and split once more as the left unit marched to Youngsville and Rocky Mount on the Catawba River on February 23. The men crossed Lynches Creek on March 3 and captured Cheraw on March 5. They then moved forward into North Carolina.

The right contingent had been busy itself. It marched northeastward out of Savannah to Beaufort on January 16. The men worked at destroying the Savannah & Charleston between the Pocataligo and Combahee Rivers on January 29 and then at McPhersonville on January 30 and 31. On February 3, the Confederates fought back at Brightons Bridge on the Salkehatchee River, but this was merely a delaying tactic. The Yankees marched northward across Whippy Swamp on February 5 and met more resistance at the Little Salkehatchee River.

The troops then attacked Bamberg and Midway on February 7 and destroyed the South Carolina Rail Road between the two towns. The Fifteenth Corps destroyed the mainline between Bamberg and Blackville and the Seventeenth Corps worked eastward from Bamberg to the Edisto River Bridge near Midway. On February 10, they crossed the North Edisto River and captured Orangeburg on February 11. After following the SCRR line, the troops crossed the Congaree River south of Columbia and began to shell the capital from Caycee on February 16. On February 17, they recrossed the river and entered Columbia, which was already burning from fires that were said to have been set in warehouses by the retreating Confederates. More interested in looting than in securing order, the soldiers soon found the flames to be out of control and a large part of the city was destroyed, despite the best efforts of the troops to strike out the flames. In ten short days the SCRR had lost more than ninety miles of track and its three longest bridges over the Edisto, Congaree and Wateree Rivers, which were rendered useless.

THE GREENVILLE & COLUMBIA AND THE ESCAPE OF THE CSA CABINET

The Greenville & Columbia lost its terminal facilities at Columbia and some twenty miles of track along the Broad River in February of 1865. In April, a secret mission pulled the G&C into a strange race of the Confederate government, which was fleeing from the invading Federal forces. With Lee's surrender, the Confederate cabinet, treasury and President Jefferson Davis himself raced across the Carolinas from Richmond. Reaching Charlotte, they were able to use the Charlotte & South Carolina to reach Rock Hill before striking out for Greenville. From there they were transported by train to the Abbeville Branch and over that line to the county seat of Abbeville. The last cabinet meeting was held there at the courthouse and, strangely, the Confederate treasury disappeared and was never found.

DESTRUCTION ON THE CHARLOTTE & SOUTH CAROLINA

On February 20, the juggernaut began to move from Columbia north along the Charlotte & South Carolina Railroad destroying this line to Blackstock, south of Chester.

Winnsboro, north of Columbia, was where the right contingent met with the left for the first time in more than a month. The left contingent troops continued up the line to Chester, where they found more than sixty freight cars at the freight yard, unable to move north to Charlotte because of a bottleneck there. The cars and the railroad buildings at Chester were destroyed by the Federal forces, which then moved toward Cheraw.

THE KINGS MOUNTAIN RAILWAY LOSS

The short courthouse Kings Mountain Railway lost its Chester terminal when Sherman's men destroyed the sixty cars in the C&SC yards there. In addition, some troops destroyed the mainline for several miles northward before turning toward Cheraw.

CAMDEN

On February 25, the divided right contingent captured Camden and destroyed the joint SCRR and W&M rail facilities there. They then began a forced march to Cheraw, which was taken in a joint action with the left contingent on March 5.

Together, Sherman's men moved on north into North Carolina while once more a group broke off and worked south along the Cheraw & Darlington to attack Florence. The troops destroyed rails and property along the C&D and arrived at Florence just as the troops from Wilmington arrived.

THE ATTACK AT AIKEN

In February of 1865, Sherman ordered General H.J. Kilpatrick to march to Graniteville near Aiken to destroy the cotton mill there, one of the first to be built in South Carolina, having been established in 1845. Confederate General Joe Wheeler met Kilpatrick and his forces on a main street of Aiken, on which the mainline of the South Carolina Rail Road was laid. Here, during the battle in which Kilpatrick and his troops were defeated, a SCRR train approached Aiken from Hamburg, unaware of the situation. Running the train almost into the midst of the hand-to-hand fighting before he became aware of what was happening, the engineer quickly reversed the train and scurried back to the safety of Graniteville where the engine, cars and goods were safe from the hands of Sherman's men.

MOVING RAILROAD EQUIPMENT OVER THE NORTH EASTERN

The SCRR had been forewarned and had sent trainloads of engines and cars east to Charleston from Hamburg to empty the line of useful equipment. The trains were then sent north over the North Eastern and the Cheraw & Darlington to Cheraw in northern South Carolina to protect the equipment from the troops. At the same time, Charleston was evacuated by rail on February 17 and the railroad terminal there was burned. Sixteen locomotives belonging to the South Carolina Rail Road and the Charleston & Savannah, as well as more than 150 cars of the SCRR, were used in this movement to Florence. Much of the equipment was then sent north over the C&D to Cheraw for protection. To secure the line and prevent Sherman's forces from following the North Eastern, the CSA torched the Santee River Bridge near St. Stephens after the last train had passed. Aside from this and the loss of terminal facilities at Charleston and Florence, the North Eastern suffered relatively little damage and was soon restored after the war ended.

Action on the Wilmington & Manchester

The Wilmington & Manchester Railroad was cut from the South Carolina Rail Road when the Wateree River Bridge was torched by the CSA to stop Sherman's advance toward Sumter in February of 1865. When joint Federal naval and marine forces captured Wilmington, North Carolina, on February 22, the locomotives that had been stored at Cheraw were rushed back to Florence and westward over the Wilmington & Manchester to the Camden Branch, where they were hidden in the Wateree Swamp north of the site of Manchester. The CSA had the bridge over the Little Pee Dee River fired to slow the advance of Union forces from Wilmington headed to Florence. However, Florence was attacked on March 5 by Yankee forces that reduced the railroad terminal to rubble and eliminated the town as a railroad junction.

Sherman's troops reached Columbia on February 17 and began to fire on the city from Cayce, across the river. In ten short days more than ninety miles of track—forty from the Edisto River Bridge to Windsor and fifty from Orangeburg to Columbia—had been destroyed and the three longest bridges on the South Carolina Rail Road had been burned to uselessness. The only undisturbed sections of the railroad were the Branchville to Charleston section, the line from Windsor to Hamburg and the Camden Branch from Manchester north.

A Diary of the Time

Mary Boykin Chesnut, the wife of United States Senator James Chesnut (who served in the Senate from 1859 to 1861 and afterward was aide to Jefferson Davis and brigadier-general in the Confederate army), wrote *A Diary from Dixie*, which was published in 1905. In the final pages, she tells of staying in Lincolnton, North Carolina, while her husband was still at Columbia as Sherman's troops arrived.

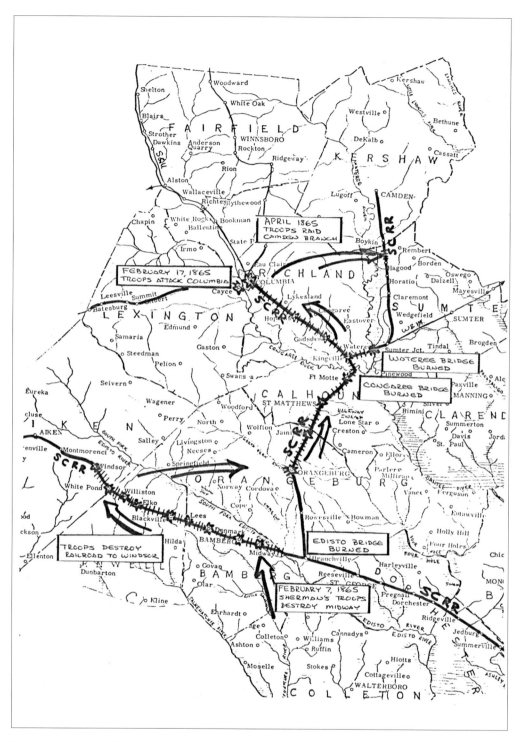

Troop movements of Sherman's army as it moved across South Carolina from early February to late April of 1865. The destruction of the South Carolina Rail Road tracks is clearly shown. *Map by author.*

She received a letter from him at Charlotte with this news.

He came near being taken a prisoner in Columbia, for he was asleep the morning of the 17th, when the Yankees blew up the railroad depot. That woke him, of course, and he found everybody had left Columbia and the town was surrendered by the mayor, Colonel Goodwyn. Hampton and his command had been gone several hours. Isaac Hayne came away with General Chesnut. There was no fire in the town when they left.

They overtook Hampton's command at Meek's Mill. That night, from the hills where they encamped, they saw the fire and knew the Yankees were burning the town as we had every reason to expect they would.

Charleston and Wilmington have surrendered. Wade Hampton has been made a lieutenant-general, too late. If he had been made one and given command in South Carolina six months ago, I believe he would have saved us.

This is all that remained of the South Carolina Rail Road offices in Columbia after the April 1865 fire swept across the city as Sherman's men entered. The source of the fire remains contentious, but many believe it was deliberately set, while the U.S. Army took pains to deny the possibility of this being their responsibility. *Author's collection.*

133

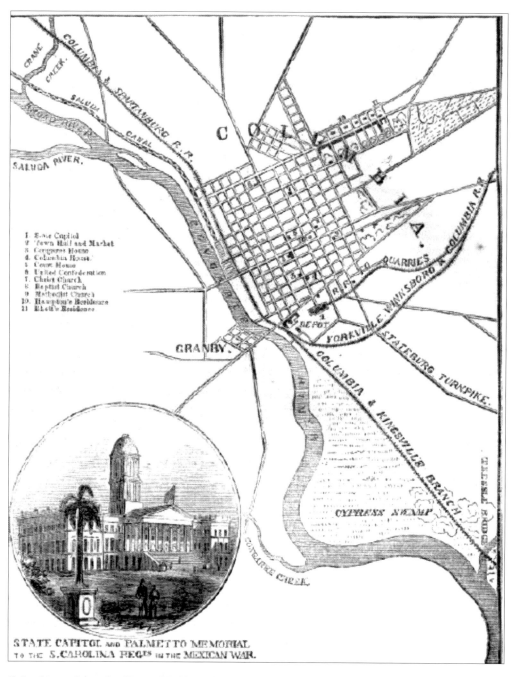

1. State Capitol
2. Town Hall and Market
3. Congress House
4. Columbia House
5. Court House
6. United Confederation
7. Christ Church
8. Baptist Church
9. Methodist Church
10. Hampton's Residence
11. Eliot's Residence

STATE CAPITOL AND PALMETTO MEMORIAL TO THE S.CAROLINA REG'S IN THE MEXICAN WAR.

Columbia, as drawn by *Harper's Weekly*, showing the railroads with the best possible names: Columbia & Spartanburg for the Greenville & Columbia; Columbia & Kingsville Branch for the South Carolina Rail Road; and Yorkville, Winnsboro & Columbia for the Charlotte & South Carolina. Note the depot very near the statehouse that was under construction using a railroad spur, "Railroad to Quarries," to bring in rock from the Rockton area near Winnsboro. *Author's collection.*

Mary told in her March 27 entry of hearing from Mrs. Prioleau Hamilton, who told of her flight from Columbia.

> *Before we left home, Major Hamilton spread a map of the United States on the table and showed me with his finger where Sherman was likely to go. Womanlike, I demurred. "But suppose he does not choose to go that way?" "Pooh Pooh! What do you know of war?"*
>
> *So we set out, my husband and myself and two children all in one small buggy. The 14th of February we took up our line of march and straight before Sherman's men for five weeks we fled together.*
>
> *The first night their beauty sleep was rudely broken into at Alston with a cry, "Move on, the Yanks are upon us!" So they hurried on, half awake, to Winnsboro, but with no better luck. Here they lightened the buggy as the Yankees were only five miles behind. They rode on to Lancaster, but Sherman was expected there and they moved east to Cheraw clearly out of the track. However at twelve o'clock, General Hardee himself knocked us up with word to "March! March!" for all the blue bonnets are over the border. They then made for Fayetteville in North Carolina where they learned that this was the seat of war now. Turning about, they headed for Chester.*

Mary had escaped to Lincolnton, North Carolina, in the high hills of western Carolina by March of 1865 and then, getting a letter from her husband asking her to return to Chester, South Carolina, she headed by train back to Charlotte. She went to the Charlotte & South Carolina depot to catch the morning train. "Arrived at the station, we had another disappointment; the train was behind time. There we sat on our boxes nine long hours, for the cars might come at any moment and we dared not move an inch from the spot. Finally the train rolled in overloaded with paroled prisoners, but heaven helped us, a kind mail agent invited us with two other forlorn women into his comfortable and clean mail-car." Her husband was waiting at the Chester station and they drove to his quarters.

GENERAL POTTER'S ASSIGNMENT

When General Sherman was advised of the escape of the valuable railroad rolling stock, he ordered General Edward E. Potter and 2,500 men to march from Georgetown on the coast to the Sumter district. "Those cars and locomotives should be destroyed if to do it cost you 500 men!"

The expeditionary force, under Potter, reached Wateree Junction in April and set fire to the trestle and destroyed five locomotives and thirteen cars. The troops also burned the turntable and the water tower, as well as a supply warehouse at that location. Proceeding on up the Camden Branch, Potter's men found and set fire to three locomotives and a long string of thirty-five freight cars.

Farther up the line at Middletown, Potter found the treasure that the Confederates so wanted him not to discover. Here were 16 locomotives and 245 passenger and freight

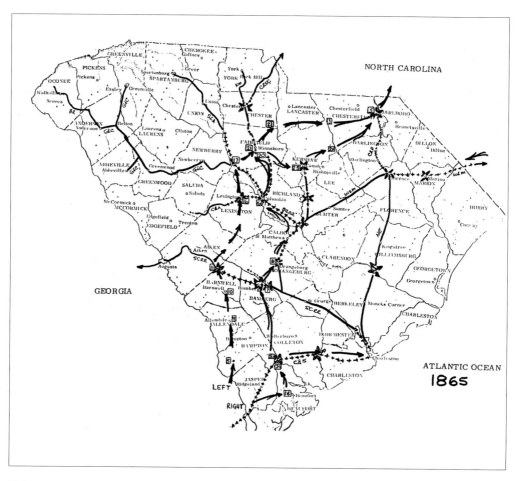

This map shows a statewide view of the troop movements and railroad destruction by Sherman's forces, as well as troops entering from Wilmington in a pincer movement. Surprisingly, the North Eastern Railroad escaped with only damage from a Union foray up the Santee River from near Georgetown to destroy the railroad bridge. *Map by author.*

cars gathered on the mainline, all within two miles of each other. All of this equipment was gleefully set to the torch and destroyed, even though ten days earlier at a courthouse called Appomattox on April 9, 1865, General Robert E. Lee had surrendered and the War of Secession was over. This final crushing blow to the South Carolina Rail Road was actually a postwar mishap because of poor communications to the field. General Potter had not been told the war was over.

SUMMARY

The growth of the rail network in South Carolina was stopped cold by the destruction of most of the railroads by the Federal forces, particularly in the final three months of

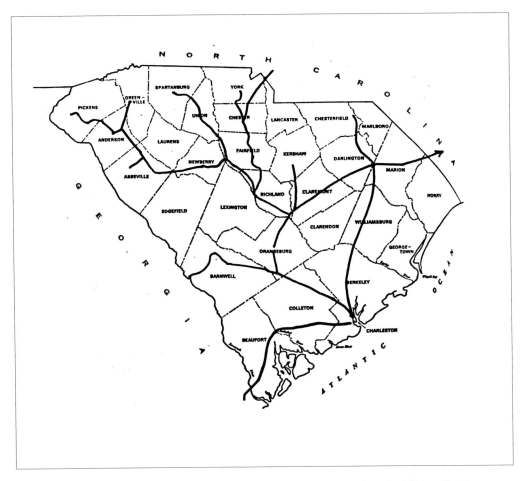

The actual political subdivisions of South Carolina before 1895 were significantly different. For the readers' benefit, all of the maps use the county designations that existed after the constitution of 1895. However, for accuracy, this map shows the railroads superimposed over the political map of the South Carolina Election Districts in 1865, which were equivalent to the county system in use today. *Map by author.*

the war. The next five years were hampered by the Reconstruction government that was installed by the Union army during its occupation, but more significantly, by the loss of the cotton shipments from plantations that were now moribund. The central plan was to restore the rail network as quickly as possible. Overall, this ten-year moratorium in rail expansion set the industry back on its heels.

South Carolina had lost 12,922 men in the war, which was equivalent to a 23 percent loss of its arms-bearing population. This was a loss greater than that of any other state and compares to a 10 percent loss of all Confederate armies and a 5 percent loss of all Union armies. This loss of actual and prospective breadwinners plus the collapse of the financial resources of the state retarded industrial development at the start of the Industrial Revolution and affected growth in the state for several generations.

1865–1870 – Rebuilding of the South Carolina Rail Road

T he shock of the loss of the war, the fall of the Confederate government and the restoration of Federal control over the Southern states led to a limbo for some five years, during which little change was made to the nature of the rail network in South Carolina. The South Carolina Rail Road, which had purchased no locomotives since June of 1860, emerged from the war with four working locomotives and thirty-five freight cars remaining on the roster. The company was permitted to restore operations on the very short Augusta to Aiken route, where the trackage had escaped damage. With no outlet to Charleston, the line could only shuttle supplies between Aiken and Augusta.

UNITED STATES MILITARY RAILROAD

Meanwhile, the longer Charleston to Orangeburg line was taken over and operated by the U.S. Military Railroad, an arm of the Union army. The first train to Orangeburg ran on May 19, 1865, and the troops found the right-of-way overgrown with marsh grass, which made the going practically impossible beyond Branchville. They reported the line was "so weed-choked that the drivers slipped as if greased." The operation by the military was short-lived and the property was returned to the South Carolina Rail Road.

RE-EQUIPPING THE LINE

The SCRR computed that its loss during the war from operations of the Federal military forces amounted to $1,438,142. In addition, the losses due to the collapse of the Confederate States of America were an additional $3,803,917, which included the loss of 111 emancipated slaves, uncollected transportation charges and defaulted bonds issued by the CSA. By summer of 1865, much of the original line was reopened and the SCRR leased seven locomotives of the Charleston & Savannah's original twelve, as well as thirty-eight cars from that line. The Charleston & Savannah had been obliterated by a splinter group of Sherman's forces as it marched to Charleston following the railroad line. Somehow, this equipment had escaped over the Ashley River Bridge, remained hidden from Potter's troops and survived.

Things were better by the end of the year. The SCRR had 44 locomotives on the property: 5 in service in the Charleston area, 1 shifting, 1 in road service, 2 between the Edisto River and Augusta, 11 on the Charlotte road (Charlotte & South Carolina), 19 awaiting repairs and 5 under repair. The company condemned 7 of the locomotives, purchased 9 new locomotives and rebuilt 1 in the shop, for a new total of 47. The line had 280 cars at the end of 1865 and condemned 4 second-class passenger cars, 5 boxcars and 6 platform cars.

The U.S. Military Railroad passed two used locomotives built by Norris to the South Carolina Rail Road in 1866. One was given the name J.W. Meridith. In addition, the company ordered four new Baldwin and three new Rogers locomotives in 1866, as they were desperate for additional motive power.

LOCOMOTIVES OF 1866

150.	no name (SCRR45)		Ex U.S. Military RR
151.	J.W. Meridith (SCRR46)		Ex U.S. Military RR
152.	no name (SCRR47)	(0-4-0)	Baldwin #1492
153.	A. Simonds (SCRR48)	(4-4-0)	Baldwin #1505
154.	John Caldwell (SCRR49)	(4-4-0)	Baldwin #1506
155.	no name (SCRR50)	(4-4-0)	Baldwin #1507
156.	Stonewall (SCRR51)		Rogers
157.	R.E. Lee (SCRR52)		Rogers
158.	T.W. Wagner (SCRR53)		Rogers

During 1866, the South Carolina Rail Road purchased 1 new passenger car, 1 boxcar and 7 platform cars and built 6 passenger cars, 3 second-class passenger cars, 42 boxcars and 53 platform cars, for a total of 377 cars on the line in good order at the end of 1866. At the same time, they had under construction in the Charleston shops 2 additional passenger cars, 2 second-class passenger cars and 16 boxcars. The company had plans to continue adding 10 cars each month through the next year.

The "new" passenger car appears to have been a coach of iron panels built by Merrick, Hanna & Company just before the war. Originally sold for $3600 each, at least one was confiscated by the U.S. Military Railroad for use on the captured rails and was then sold to the South Carolina Rail Road in 1866 as surplus property. Based on the construction from iron, this car was the most experimental passenger car on the line, and likely the heaviest to operate between Charleston and Columbia.

By the end of 1866, the road reported that trains were finally able to reach Columbia on January 16, 1866, after replacing the bridges. The company also ran through from Charleston to Augusta on April 5 for the first time since the war had ended. The terminal buildings at Columbia were found to be secure even though they had been burned when the city was torched. The company rebuilt them in place, although the

The iron coach acquired by the South Carolina Rail Road in 1866 was provided by the U.S. Military Railroad that had appropriated it from the Pittsburgh, Fort Wayne and Chicago Railroad, along with two others. It is seen here about 1893, when in service hauling workers to the Charleston Mining & Manufacturing Co. plant at Lambs on the Ashley River, near Magnolia Gardens. *Author's collection.*

freight depot was extended another 50 feet to accommodate the increased shipments of cotton. A second freight depot, 150 feet long by 40 feet wide, was built for joint use with the Greenville & Columbia Railroad.

In Augusta, the company's property had not been damaged. However, they found that they needed a suitable shed to be erected along Reynolds Street to provide shelter for the passenger trains that were "lying over at this point."

Charleston needed extensive repair of the cotton yards, which were planked-over areas served by a number of sidings in the area between King and Meeting Streets north of St. John in the city. Besides replanking the area, a number of shelters had to be provided to reduce exposure to inclement weather.

The railroad was forced to "re-iron" the track with old lightweight rails, and this forced the SCRR to operate at a reduced, moderate speed. The schedules were rearranged to provide a new through train from Augusta to Columbia via Branchville that had connections on to Charleston. Another new train left Charleston and split at Branchville to run to both Augusta and Columbia. This ploy saved the service of three engines and nine cars that had been needed under the original schedules. In addition, the Columbia to Augusta train provided a part of a through service in agreement with "the Railroad Companies on the line between New York and New Orleans" and was to run for at least six months, from October of 1866 to April of 1867. This was the first coordinated attempt to provide a through passenger service across the Eastern half of the country, although gauge changes forced the traveling passenger to change from car to car at the different terminals of the cooperating lines.

A tri-weekly train was operated on the Camden Branch as far as Sanders, the temporary end of the line because of the extensive damage in the Wateree Swamp from Potter's men destroying the equipment during the days following the war. In addition, most of the rails beyond Sanders, some fifteen miles, had been removed to rebuild the Columbia division. This was to be replaced in 1867, and indeed, was complete by May of that year.

The rails that were removed proved to be "entirely too light for the heavy trains, particularly on the steep grades, and should be taken up and 56 pound rails put in their stead, for which purpose ten miles should be had the coming year." The Edisto Bridge and trestle at the Edisto River was reported to be frequently endangered by the "accumulation of rafts which require constant watching...to prevent the trestling [sic] from being swept away." This apparently refers to rafts of cut timber being sent downstream to be transported to the mills at Charleston. Near Columbia, the Congaree was going to be eliminated as a slow speed barrier by having a new bridge installed by the end of April 1867.

Finally, the Wilmington & Manchester Railroad kept up the joint occupancy of the 8⅓ miles between Kingville and Manchester Junction and provided a beneficial connection to Sumter over their line.

In 1868, passenger service over the South Carolina Rail Road consisted of a morning train out of Charleston to Augusta and Columbia, and two trains from Augusta and Columbia toward Branchville bound for Charleston. Columbia was reached in nine and a half hours, and Augusta was reached in exactly nine hours. The Camden Branch was under a W&M timetable with a direct connection to and from the Charleston train at Kingville. The thirty-eight miles through to Camden were covered in two and a half hours.

The last named locomotive purchased by the SCRR was the Ashley, a Rogers locomotive obtained in 1868. This replaced the old SCRR #33, the S. Miles, a 4-6-0 Baldwin, which was worn out.

LOCOMOTIVE OF 1868

159. Ashley (SCRR33, second)   replaced #33

Severely impacted by lack of income and yet hampered by the lack of good locomotives, the company purchased one Baldwin 4-4-0 in November of 1869 from Baird & Company, the new name for the Baldwin Locomotive manufacturing plant.

LOCOMOTIVE OF 1869

160. no name (SCRR54)   (4-4-0)   Baird & Company

COMPETITION: COLUMBIA & AUGUSTA RAILROAD, 1863

A new railroad, the Columbia & Augusta Railroad, had been chartered in 1863 to form a more direct route between Columbia and Augusta, a route critical to the Confederate States of America. Some twenty miles were built from Cayce, across the Broad River from Columbia, to Batesburg, but the entire line was destroyed by Sherman's troops just before the siege on Columbia. Construction on the line began again shortly after the end of the war.

The South Carolina Rail Road looked on this construction as infringing on the original South Carolina charter, which granted exclusive rights to connect Hamburg and Columbia by rail (although through Branchville). In June of 1867, the SCRR moved a train onto the proposed rail crossing of the interloper, but the city of Columbia forced the crew to move their train under threat of arrest. The Columbia & Augusta immediately rushed in a track gang and completed the crossing, but two days later, the SCRR sent its own track gang to the area to tear out the crossing. The men succeeded in removing the crossing, but they were arrested for their efforts. The disagreement went to court, where it was settled in favor of the Columbia & Augusta in December of 1867 and the crossing was replaced to stay.

The new railroad reached Warrensville in Horse Creek Valley, very close to Augusta, in 1869. Realizing the potential of this new line, the Charlotte & South Carolina gained control over the Columbia & Augusta that same year and merged to become the new Charlotte, Columbia & Augusta Railroad. Initially, the new company arranged to use the tracks of the South Carolina Rail Road from Warrensville on into Augusta over the SCRR Bridge at Hamburg.

EXTENSION: KINGS MOUNTAIN RAILWAY, 1865

The Kings Mountain Railroad lacked the funds to rebuild the line after the war ended. The company was reorganized as the Kings Mountain Railway late in 1865 to rebuild its terminal at Chester and replace the track that had been destroyed north of Chester.

COMPETITION: SAVANNAH & CHARLESTON RAILROAD, 1866

A new company, the Savannah & Charleston, was chartered at the end of 1866. The S&C purchased the wrecked and abandoned track and right-of-way of the former Charleston & Savannah Railroad and began to rebuild the line. The new railroad was completed in 1869, but lacked the rail connection over the Ashley River that the Confederacy had built in 1864. The northern terminal of the S&C was in Saint Andrews Parish and freight and passengers were hauled by wagon or stagecoach to the rail connections in Charleston using the Ashley River Bridge, which lacked any rails.

EXTENSION: SPARTANBURG & ASHEVILLE, 1868

Despite the natural barriers that lay on the route, a new railroad, the Spartanburg & Asheville, was chartered in 1868. However, there was no public response to the call for funds to build the line and no work was started until 1876 in this second attempt to cross the Blue Ridge Mountains.

COMPETITION: CHARLOTTE, COLUMBIA & AUGUSTA RAILROAD, 1870

The new company that had combined the Charlotte & South Carolina with the Columbia & Augusta as the Charlotte, Columbia & Augusta Railroad completed its line to Augusta in 1870, providing a through route from the North Carolina railways at Charlotte directly to the Georgia railways at Augusta. The company built its own covered bridge across the Savannah River a little more than a block upstream of the South Carolina Rail Road Bridge.

Two years later the company formed an agreement with the Wilmington, Columbia & Augusta to handle the WC&A trains through to Augusta. This gave the CC&A two routes east from Augusta: one to Charlotte to the north and one via the WC&A to Wilmington on the Atlantic Ocean.

COMPETITION: THE WILMINGTON, COLUMBIA & AUGUSTA RAILROAD, 1870

The Wilmington & Manchester Railroad was bankrupt and unable to recover from the war damages. Although it managed to run some trains, the company was barely able to hang on. William T. Walters of Baltimore had sympathized with the CSA and lived in Europe during the war. When he returned he began to buy connected short lines to form a new Atlantic Coast Line Fast Mail Passenger Route between Weldon, North Carolina, and Columbia, South Carolina. He bought the Wilmington & Manchester in 1870 using his Wilmington, Columbia & Augusta Railroad to complete the transaction. The WC&A then built a new forty-three-mile extension from Sumter directly toward Columbia and when the line was completed in 1872, dissolved the joint ownership of the SCRR's Camden Branch. It also abandoned its own track in 1872 from Sumter to Manchester Junction, where it had connected with the South Carolina Rail Road. Manchester was abandoned and the inhabitants moved to Wedgefield, where the new WC&A crossed the Camden Branch.

This new construction presented a loss of through passenger business over the South Carolina Rail Road from Sumter and points east, to the SCRR terminal at Augusta via Branchville. The Sumter service was now through routed over the new WC&A route directly to Columbia and then over the new Charlotte, Columbia & Augusta directly to Augusta.

William Walters had the WC&A purchase the Wilmington & Weldon in November of 1872 to make a connection with coastal steamboats at the port of Suffolk, Virginia, well to the north of Wilmington. These ships provided direct service to Washington, Baltimore, Philadelphia and New York.

The state entered the 1870s with one new rail line between Columbia and Augusta and with all the remaining lines restored to operation, with the single exception of the Laurens Railroad, which had its rails confiscated by the CSA. Northern capitalists were now beginning to look seriously at developing the railroads in the South into connected systems and several South Carolina routes looked very promising for this type of development.

THE NUMBERED FLEET OF LOCOMOTIVES

Since the South Carolina Rail Road stopped the naming of locomotives with the Ashley, which was the second machine with #33, except that the original had been the M.W. Baldwin, it can be seen why keeping tabs on the machines had to be simplified by using only numbers. This list is the SCRR locomotives by number.

Some study of the list will show that the longest lifespan of a locomotive was thirty-one years, and the shortest was only ten years. Locomotives built by Rogers provided the best chance to get a long life from a machine.

#	BUILDER	NAME (IF ANY)	BUILT	SCRAPPED	YEARS
7	Norris	Joseph Johnson	1852	1880	28
8	Norris	Wm. Aiken	1852	1871	19
9	Norris	Governor Manning	1853	1870	18
10	Norris	W.H. Thomas	1853	1879	26
11	Norris	Fawn	1854	1871	17
12	Baldwin	Governor Morehead	1854	1874	20
13	Norris	Mayor Hutchinson	1854	1871	17
14	Norris	Mitchell King	1854	1880	26
15	Norris	Ariel	1851	1872	21
16	Norris	Wade Hampton	1853		
17	RK&G	Thomas Rogers	1855	1884	29
18	Baldwin	James Gadsden	1855	1886	31
19	Baldwin	G.B. Lythgoe	1855	1870	15
19 (2nd)	Rogers			1875	
20	Norris	C.M. Furman	1855	1886	31
21	RK&G	William C. Dukes	1856	1886	30
22	RK&G	Henry Gourdin	1856	1886	30
23	RK&G	L.J. Patterson	1856	1886	30
24	Baldwin	John Bryce	1856	1873	17
24 (2nd)	SCRR			1873	
25	Baldwin	James Rose	1856	1886	30
26	Norris	T. Tupper	1856	1871	15
26 (2nd)	SCRR		1873		
27	Norris	George A. Trenholm	1856	1884	28

#	BUILDER	NAME (IF ANY)	BUILT	SCRAPPED	YEARS
28	Baldwin	Governor Adams	1856		
29	Baldwin	Sam Tate	1857	(sold 1900)	
30	Norris	Preston S. Brooks	1857	1871	14
30 (2nd)	BPW&Co.			1873	
31	RK&G	L.M. Keitt	1857	1887	30
32	Baldwin	S. Miles	1858	1887	30
33	Baldwin	M.W. Baldwin	1858	1868	10
33 (2nd)	Rogers	Ashley		1868	
34	RK&G	James S. Scott	1858	1886	28
35	Baldwin	Thomas Waring	1859	1876	17
36	Baldwin	W.C. Gatewood	1859	1876	17
37	Baldwin	A. Burnside	1859	1876	17
38	Baldwin	E.F. Raworth	1859	1886	27
39	Baldwin	C.T. Mitchell	1859	1876	17
39 (2nd)	BPW&Co.		1877	1901	24
40	Baldwin	J.S. Corry	1859		
41	Baldwin	W.S. Stockman	1859		
42	Portland Co.		1850	(Ex SPART & UNION)	
43	Baldwin	Gen. James Simon	1860	(sold to G&C 1873)	
43 (2nd)	BPW&Co.			1875	
44	Baldwin	W.D. Porter	1860		
44 (2nd)	BPW&Co.			1875	
45	U.S. Military			(bought 1866)	
46	U.S. Military	J.W. Meridith		(bought 1866)	
47	Baldwin		1866	(sold 1900)	
48	Baldwin	A. Simonds	1866		
49	Baldwin	John Caldwell	1866		
50	Baldwin		1866		
51	Rogers	Stonewall	1866		
52	Rogers	R.E. Lee	1866		
53	Rogers	T.W. Wagner	1866		
54	Baird & Co.		1869		
55	Baird & Co.		1870		
56	Baird & Co.		1870		
57	Rogers		1870		
58	Rogers		1870		
59	SCRR		1877		

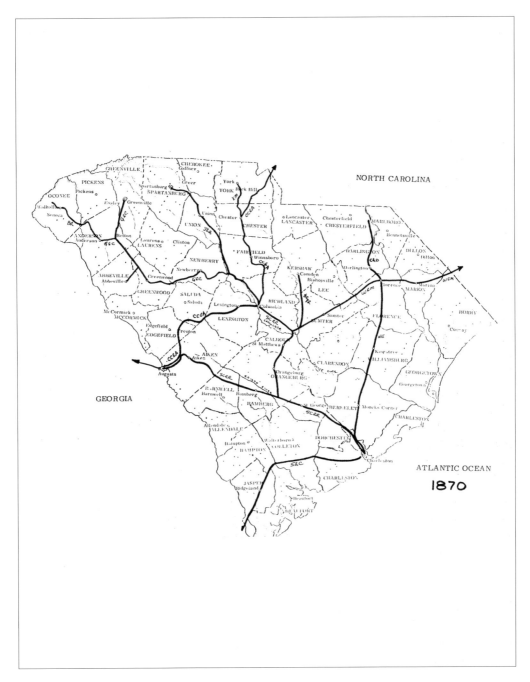

The five years after the war ended saw little change to the overall state railway system. Most of the attention was devoted to replacing the trackage that had been destroyed. The exception was the new Charlotte, Columbia & Augusta line via Lexington and Trenton to the Savannah River. *Map by author.*

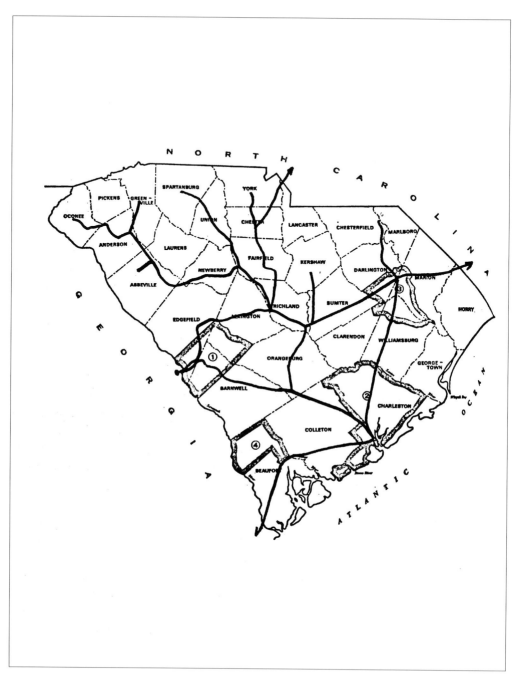

South Carolina created the following redistricting of the counties in 1868. New counties were Aiken, from parts of Edgefield, Lexington and Barnwell; Berkeley, from what had been known as both Charleston County and Berkeley County; Florence County, from parts of Marion, Williamsburg, Clarendon and Darlington Counties; and finally Hampton County, from the northern part of Beaufort County. The railroads have been superimposed on this map to show the relative locations. *Map by author.*

1870–1880–Reconstruction

For a region still suffering from the broken economy of the postwar years, the decade from 1870 to 1880 saw the construction of only two new major lines in the South Carolina rail network, completion of three narrow gauge lines that copied the economies of General Palmer's Colorado narrow gauge ventures and the bankruptcy of most of the existing independent lines. These factors gave rise to the new rail systems that were soon to control most of the state's railroads.

SOUTH CAROLINA RAIL ROAD

The South Carolina Rail Road reported in 1873 that it owned 42 locomotives, 22 first-class passenger cars, 25 second-class passenger cars and 497 freight cars. The company also owned and operated its own sleeping cars over its route. However, the company was destitute under the burden of a $6,000,000 debt and only had enough money to invest in the Greenville & Columbia Railroad. The company sold fare tickets that looked like currency and the bills were accepted as such. The units were one fare ticket for a twenty-five-mile ride.

The Reconstruction period in South Carolina placed the rail line into severe financial difficulty, and in October of 1878 the South Carolina Rail Road fell into receivership. The road found that the cost of completely rebuilding the line plus the loss of the connection to Sumter had a direct impact on the income. In addition, the huge numbers of bales of cotton shipped before the war did not return, as the plantations were unable to support themselves without the slave labor of the prewar period. Three years later, the line was purchased for $1,275,000 on July 28, 1881, by New York financiers who reorganized the line as the South Carolina Railway.

GREENVILLE & COLUMBIA, 1870

The Greenville & Columbia, which had been controlled by the State of South Carolina since 1850, was released to private ownership in 1870. In 1875 the G&C purchased the right-of-way of the Laurens Railway, which had been confiscated by the CSA, and rebuilt the track from Helena, the connection with the G&C near Newberry, through Clinton to Laurens in 1876. While not long in length, it restored service to the courthouse and the market in an area without rail service.

Wilmington & Columbia, 1870

The Wilmington & Manchester was offered for sale by the State of North Carolina, its biggest creditor, on January 5, 1870. It was purchased by the Wilmington & Columbia Railroad, which publicly operated the line as the Wilmington, Columbia & Augusta Railroad, since it offered through service over the Charlotte, Columbia & Augusta until 1873.

The Pennsylvania Southern Railway Security System, 1871–1876

The Pennsylvania Southern Railway Security System was a financial organization developed by the backers of the Pennsylvania Railroad to purchase distressed Southern railroads after the war and unite them into a regional system. Organized in 1871, the PSR was unknown to the general public (and remains much of a mystery 135 years later), but it exercised financial control over the affairs of the following South Carolina lines: Atlanta & Richmond Air Line; Charlotte, Columbia & Augusta; North Eastern; Cheraw & Darlington; and the Wilmington, Columbia & Augusta.

The construction of the Columbia & Sumter Railroad in 1871 (see below) was directed by the PSR to form a direct connection between the member roads within the state by linking Columbia with Sumter.

The PSR was broken up in 1876, but the lines maintained some of the former relationships, as is evident in the cooperation of the Atlantic Coast Line and the Richmond & Danville (later the Southern Railway System) at the expense of the independent and competitive Seaboard Air Line. The Union Stations at Charleston, Columbia and Augusta all managed to freeze out the Seaboard, which then built its own stations, or in the case of Augusta, abandoned the proposed route altogether.

It is ironic to consider that the ACL and Seaboard were to merge in the late 1900s to become the CSX arch rival of the Southern Railway in its new Norfolk Southern identity.

Competition: Columbia & Sumter, 1871

The Wilmington & Columbia formed the Columbia & Sumter Railroad to build a new forty-three-mile extension from Sumter directly to Columbia. The line was completed in January 1872 and the C&S was merged into the W&C.

The former Wilmington & Manchester line to Manchester from Sumter was immediately abandoned, as was all interest in the jointly owned Camden Branch. The South Carolina Rail Road, as a consequence, could offer service to Sumter only through a connection with the WC&A at Columbia.

North Eastern Railroad, 1875

The North Eastern Railroad came under the control of Walter's Atlantic Coast group of investors in 1875. It then became one of several lines joined in the Atlantic Coast Lines of Railroads. This was the third rail system in the Carolinas (R&D, SA-L and ACLofRR).

The Atlanta & Richmond Air Line, 1871

The first of the all-new rail routes was based on the 1856 South Carolina Air Line Railroad, which proposed to connect Greenville and Spartanburg with Charlotte. The company had graded a portion of this right-of-way before the War Between the States ended the project. The Atlanta & Richmond Air Line purchased the moribund SCAL charter and began construction west and south from Charlotte in 1871. Working through 1872, the line was completed to Atlanta by September of 1873

The A&RAL provided connections to the Spartanburg & Union at Spartanburg, the Greenville & Columbia at Greenville and the Blue Ridge Railroad at Seneca, but there was little demand for traffic along the mountains rather than straight to Charleston and the shipping facilities there.

The CC&A Becomes Standard Gauge, 1873

The track throughout South Carolina had all been built to five-foot gauge for universal interchange of rail equipment. However in 1873, the Charlotte, Columbia & Augusta was converted to standard gauge (four foot, eight and a half inches) to match the gauge of the North Carolina Railroad, owned by the State of North Carolina. This conversion eliminated any interchange of equipment between the CC&A and any other South Carolina or Georgia railway. This abruptly ended the cooperative through service of Wilmington & Columbia trains over the CC&A to Augusta.

However, the company gained direct connections northward through North Carolina and into Virginia to connect with the standard-gauge lines of the North. The CC&A lost considerable business after the conversion and was taken over by the Richmond & Danville System, which was being developed by its new owners, the Clyde Steamship Company. The R&D System was to grow to become one of the parents of the Southern Railway System.

Spartanburg & Asheville, 1876

Prevented from starting the project by lack of funds, the company was reorganized by Colonel R.Y. McAdden and work began in 1876. The tracks were laid rapidly north out of Spartanburg and reached Tryon, North Carolina, at the foot of the mountains and at the South Carolina state line, late in the year. From Tryon, the S&A carved out an ascension without tunnels using a 4.70 percent grade, the steepest mainline grade in the United States both then and now. The line was opened to the village of Saluda, at the top of Saluda Grade, in 1878. It then reached Hendersonville in 1879, where patrons could change to stagecoaches to ride on into Asheville.

THE ATLANTA & CHARLOTTE AIR LINE, 1877

The Atlanta & Richmond Air Line railroad company was forced into reorganization in 1877 and emerged as the new Atlanta & Charlotte Air Line. This company developed a through passenger and freight service with the new Seaboard Air-Line. The SA-L had been formed by combining the Seaboard & Roanoke with the Inland Air Line Route (Raleigh & Gaston Railroad). The SA-L then had leased the Carolina Central in North Carolina from Raleigh to Charlotte. Constructing connecting trackage in Charlotte, the SA-L then arranged to use the A&CAL route from Charlotte via Gastonia, North Carolina; Spartanburg and Greenville in South Carolina; and Toccoa and Gainesville in Georgia to reach Atlanta. This was the first one-ticket rail system in the South to offer through passage from Suffolk to Atlanta, but it was to be short-lived.

The Richmond & Danville, which now controlled the Charlotte, Columbia & Augusta, found the new SA-L through system intolerable and began to make plans for severing the SA-L's line to Atlanta and gaining control of the A&CAL for itself.

COMPETITION: THE PORT ROYAL LINES, 1871

The second rail system to develop was the one based on Port Royal, a port town just below Beaufort between the Coosaw and Broad Rivers on the Atlantic Coast. Port Royal had watched the development of the Charleston and Savannah ports with the use of railroads from the interior with envy, and it was not long before town members decided to replicate the concept locally.

The Port Royal Railroad had been chartered in 1856, but was unable to raise funds to begin building. After the war, outside backers were found and the line was completed from Port Royal to Yemassee on the Savannah & Charleston mainline in 1871.

GEORGIA RAILROAD "MAGNOLIA ROUTE"

Unable to continue construction for lack of funds, the Port Royal was able to get assistance from the Georgia Rail Road & Banking Company, which issued bonds for the construction in 1872. The line was put in place fairly rapidly and bridged the Savannah River about ten miles south of Augusta. This extension was opened in 1873 and was operated by the Georgia Railroad. With little income from the online businesses and practically no through freight, as Augusta shipped everything to Savannah, the Magnolia Route defaulted in November and operated in receivership into 1878, when it was sold to the Port Royal & Augusta.

PORT ROYAL & AUGUSTA

The new PR&A developed a through passenger service from Atlanta to Savannah as well as to Charleston via Augusta, Yemassee and the Savannah & Charleston Line.

COMPETITION: SAVANNAH & CHARLESTON

The Savannah & Charleston lacked through freight business, as it had no connection at Charleston and any through freight had to be teamed across the Ashley River and reloaded. The company became bankrupt in 1873 and continued to operate in receivership until 1880.

COMPETITION: ASHLEY RIVER RAILROAD, 1878

The Savannah & Charleston could no longer tolerate the lack of a connection at Charleston, especially in light of the connection that had existed in 1864 and 1865 just before the war's end. Unable to finance a bridge across the wide waters of the Ashley at Charleston, the company decided to build an all-new route following Bee's Ferry Road and to cross at Bee's Ferry where the Ashley narrowed. The route was well established, as it was in use when the first surveys of the Charleston & Hamburg had been made. As built, the new Ashley River Railroad ran from Johns Island station northeast to Bee's Ferry, across the Ashley on a draw-span, then along Dorchester Road to the Forks and along the west side of King Street to Magnolia Cemetery, where it crossed the South Carolina Rail Road to connect with the North Eastern. Savannah & Charleston trains would run south to near Calhoun Street to terminate at the North Eastern terminal.

BLUE RIDGE RAILROAD, 1873

The Blue Ridge Railroad still intrigued a number of investors. If the line could get past Stumphouse Mountain, the right-of-way crossed the Eastern Divide just north of Clayton, Georgia, with the shallowest crossing in the entire range. Construction on the tunnels in northwestern Oconee County began in earnest in 1873, but the spiraling costs ran as high as $50,000 a mile and the line was again bankrupt in 1880, without any additional route mileage to show for the money and labor poured into the Stumphouse Mountain tunnel project.

SPARTANBURG & UNION, 1879

With no connection other than to the Atlanta & Charlotte Air Line, the Spartanburg & Union wilted from lack of business and was bankrupt in 1879 for lack of business.

COMPETITION: THREE-FOOT NARROW-GAUGE LINES, 1873

Narrow-gauge lines in Colorado were the subject of much controversy in this decade. General William J. Palmer had visited the Festiniog Railway in Wales, which used the odd gauge of 1 foot, 11½ inches (23½ inches). He returned and proposed to build a new railroad form Denver to Mexico City using a new 3-foot gauge for the track. This Denver & Rio Grande began construction in early 1871 and the first trains were running over the first few miles out of Denver in August, which made the D&RG the first narrow-gauge common carrier in the United States.

The initial success with the smaller roadbed, sharper curves and steeper grades— which all served to lower construction costs—led to duplication in South Carolina. Three railroads were built to Palmer's three-foot narrow gauge.

CHERAW & SALISBURY RAILROAD, 1873

The first of these narrow-gauge railroads was the Cheraw & Salisbury Railroad, which ran north from Cheraw to Wadesboro, North Carolina. Chartered in 1857, the line was partially graded by the CSA in 1864 in an effort to move North Carolina coal to the naval ships at Charleston. The line was opened in 1873 for the twenty-three miles connecting the five-foot Carolina Central in North Carolina to the five-foot Cheraw & Darlington at Cheraw. Freight and passengers were forced to change cars at each terminal to continue their journey.

CHESTER & LENOIR NARROW-GAUGE RAILROAD, 1874

The Chester & Lenoir narrow-gauge railroad was chartered in 1873 and opened from Chester to York in 1874. The line purchased the existing Kings Mountain Railway and re-gauged it to three feet between the rails. Construction northward reached Lincolnton, North Carolina, north of Gastonia, in 1880.

The line terminated at Chester with a connection to the standard-gauge Charlotte, Columbia & Augusta and midway crossed the Atlanta & Charlotte's five-foot gauge line at Gastonia, North Carolina. At each point, passengers were forced to reboard cars of the C&LNG to continue and all freight had to be reloaded.

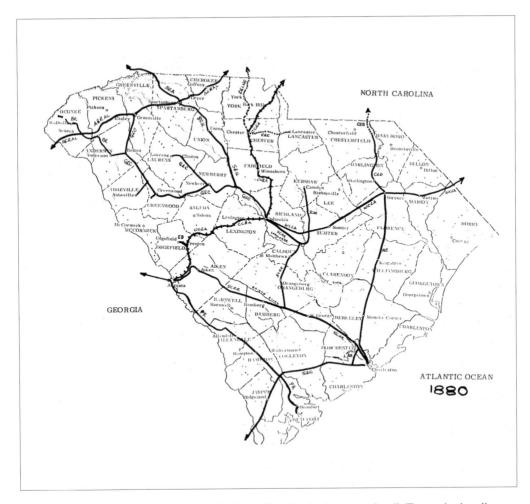

At the beginning of 1880, the rail system in South Carolina had recovered well. Two major handicaps appeared, however, as the Charlotte, Columbia & Augusta converted to the North Carolina standard gauge, which eliminated any freight interchange of equipment in South Carolina or in Augusta; and the construction of two three-foot gauge lines out of Chester, known as the Cheraw & Lancaster narrow-gauge Railroad and the Chester & Cheraw Railroad. A new line ran from Augusta to Port Royal, but was quickly pulled into control by one or the other Georgia lines. *Map by author.*

CHERAW & CHESTER, 1880

Chartered in 1873, the Cheraw & Chester opened in 1880 from Chester to Lancaster. Designed to connect with the Cheraw & Salisbury at Cheraw, and the Chester & Lenoir narrow-gauge at Chester, the little C&C was unable to complete the mainline beyond Lancaster.

COMPETITION: GREENWOOD & AUGUSTA, 1879

The Greenwood & Augusta Railroad was chartered in 1879 and began construction south from Greenwood, on the Greenville & Columbia line. It soon ground to a halt for lack of sufficient funds. This was the first of several companies to become interested in the route, but the G&A was soon forgotten.

COMPETITION: EDGEFIELD BRANCH RAILROAD, 1879

The Edgefield Branch Railroad was another of the common courthouse lines run from the mainline to a local courthouse district. Formed by the Charlotte, Columbia & Augusta, the six-mile line from Trenton ran north to Edgefield.

SUMMARY

The initial formation of the three narrow-gauge rail systems during the decade was a signal for intensive competitive building and the purchase of independent lines to strengthen the systems at the expense of other lines. The bankruptcy of so many South Carolina independent railroads was to aid the formation of the rail systems as no other incident could have done.

   The national rail system was to remember this decade as that of its greatest growth, as the mileage sprang from 53,000 miles in 1870 to 93,000 miles in 1880. But it remained up to the next decade for the Carolina lines to suddenly spring forward once more.

Epilogue

The advent of the Southern Railway in South Carolina changed things dramatically as lines were purchased or leased and allegiances were shifted accordingly. That is the subject for another book, although most of the available books on the Southern Railway tend to be coffee table photo essays, not histories.

Few people know how close the states came to war when President Buchanan sent the *Star of the West* to Charleston to resupply Fort Sumter using a commercial steamship with troops and munitions hidden below deck—a sort of Trojan horse. Citadel Cadets at Morris Island, alerted by telegraph of the duplicity, fired on the ship and turned it back. Major Anderson's decision not to return fire from Fort Sumter, since Sumter was not under attack, prevented the flare-up of war in January of 1861. Nevertheless, war came only three months later.

The war was devastating to the South Carolina railroads. Rebuilding the lines, while done with persistence, nevertheless led to bankruptcy, or foreclosure and reorganization in a new company with more ambitious plans and new capital.

The formation of new railroad systems began to link small and mid-size independent roads into larger and larger networks that sought to provide one-ticket rides from Washington and Richmond to Chattanooga, Atlanta, New Orleans and Jacksonville. We have seen how some of these smaller mergers were not well thought out and ran from nowhere to nowhere without the benefit of a major terminal junction or port city.

This journey is over, but there are many other stories to be told of the other South Carolina railroads. After all, when Charleston lost control of the South Carolina Rail Road to the state government, the city backed the new North Eastern up to Florence, a story most worthy in its own right.

About the Author

T om Fetters lives in Lombard, Illinois, on the mainline of the Union Pacific (C&NW), twenty miles west of Chicago. After graduating from the High School of Charleston and earning a BS in chemical engineering at Clemson University, he moved north to Chicago to work for Continental Can and Crown Cork & Seal. His work often required trips to Spartanburg, Birmingham, Atlanta and New Orleans, as well as Europe and South America. He often used his spare time to search the local libraries in the South for railroad material that turned out to be unique source material for his books.

He received a commendation from the South Carolina House of Representatives in June of 1995 for preserving the railroad history of the state.

Visit us at
www.historypress.net